LIFE IN
GEORGIAN ENGLAND

Master and pupils

Life in
GEORGIAN ENGLAND

E. N. WILLIAMS

English Life Series
Edited by PETER QUENNELL

LONDON: B. T. BATSFORD LTD
NEW YORK: G. P. PUTNAM'S SONS

First published 1962

© E. N. Williams, 1962

Made and printed in Great Britain
by William Clowes and Sons, Limited, London and Beccles
for the publishers
B. T. BATSFORD LTD
4 Fitzhardinge Street, Portman Square, London, W.1
G. P. PUTNAM'S SONS
200 Madison Avenue, New York 16, N.Y.

To
My Mother
and Father

By the same author

THE EIGHTEENTH-CENTURY CONSTITUTION

Preface

My debt to the chief historians of eighteenth-century England will be evident on every page. Since it has not been thought suitable to quote sources in a work of this nature, my first duty is to thank (and apologise to) those authorities whose works I have ransacked. To one of these I am especially grateful, and that is Dr J. H. Plumb, whose criticisms have been invaluable, and whose kindness inexhaustible. Messrs Michael Langley-Webb and Harry Pitt have also read the manuscript and made valuable suggestions. I am particularly grateful to them for their frank comments. I am also indebted to Mr Donald Bradfield and Mr Bert Howard for their warm encouragement; and to Mr Basil Cridland, who saved me from a number of errors in one section. Above all, I must thank my pupils, who teach me my history.

Dulwich   E. N. W.
Spring 1962

Contents

Acknowledgment

The illustration on page 147 is reproduced by gracious permission of Her Majesty the Queen.

The author and publishers wish to thank the following for the illustrations appearing in this book: The Ashmolean Museum, Oxford for page 32; the Trustees of the British Museum for page 43; the Dulwich Gallery for page 28; Lord Durham for page 64; the Trustees of the Goodwood Collection for pages 7, 8 (top) and 100; Lady Hudson for page 23; Lord Mountbatten for page 94 (bottom); the Trustees of the National Gallery for page 45; the National Galleries of Scotland for page 40; the National Portrait Gallery for pages 6, 67, 68, 123, 131, 138, 141, 151, 161, and 166; Lord Northbrook for page 74; Lord O'Hagen for page 159; the Parker Gallery for page 38; *Radio Times* Hulton Picture Library for page 81; the Rothampstead Experimental Station, Harpenden for page 17; the Royal Academy of Arts for page 94 (bottom); Sport and General for page 70; the Trustees of the Tate Gallery for pages 34 and 136; the Trustees of the Victoria and Albert Museum (Crown Copyright Reserved) for pages 48 and 144; the Walker Art Gallery, Liverpool for page 110; the Marquess of Zetland for page 33.

List of Illustrations

xi

xii

LIST OF ILLUSTRATIONS

xiv

I

The English People

Perhaps the most important single development in eighteenth-century England was the growth of population, but the most astonishing feature to us looking back is the way the numbers then are dwarfed by the figures now. It is like looking at England through the wrong end of a telescope. When William III and Marlborough defeated Louis XIV, the population of England and Wales was about five and three-quarter million: not much more than the present population of Middlesex, Kent and Surrey combined. About twice the numbers at present governed by the London County Council sufficed under Chatham to defeat France and conquer Canada and half India: six and a half million. And at the end of the century just over nine million brought Napoleon down and made England the most powerful state in the world. This is a good deal less than the joint population of present-day Lancashire and Yorkshire. Nor is that the whole story, for the population of our chief enemy was not similarly reduced. On each of those occasions, the people of France were a Goliath, three times the English size.

Of course, there is a good deal of guess-work about these numbers. Until the census of 1801 they are only estimates. Although the eighteenth century is the first to make statistically-minded historians happy with a rich range of hard figures from which to draw graphs of industrial production, shipping turnover or food prices, their picture of the population-increase necessarily contains much guess-work—some of it very ingenious. The most valuable estimator of all was Gregory King whose total of five and a half million for the year 1696 is still regarded as

1

being about right by later calculators. King's work, which was not printed till 1801, contains the most fascinating detail. His break-down of the various occupations and classes, for example, shows that England contained, in part, 160 temporal lords, 26 spiritual lords, 12,000 gentlemen, 15,000 'persons in liberal arts and sciences', 50,000 shopkeepers and tradesmen, 364,000 'labouring people and outservants' and 849,000 'vagrants: as gipsies, thieves, beggars, etc.'. The total acreage of each of the various types of landscape is given, such as arable land, pasture, woods, rivers, lakes, meres and ponds; and he calculated that these supported, among other things, twelve million sheep and lambs and two million rabbits and conies. No method has so far been devised of confirming or denying his rabbit figures. He expected the (human) population to rise, and his guess for the year 1900 was 7,350,000; which was a better shot than most diviners of the eighteenth century would have made, for the general feeling, oddly enough, was that the population was going down. A chance of finding out was lost in 1753 when Parliament rejected a proposal to take a census. Opponents of the scheme said that it would reveal England's weakness to the enemy, or that it would bring down divine displeasure, or (a conclusive argument in the Georgian period) that it was sub-versive of individual liberty. Consequently, we have no hard figures till the first census of 1801, and even that has to have an estimate of the soldiers, sailors and marines built into it before it is sound—for they were away at the war.

This puny but pugnacious people was spread over the face of the country in a much more even way than it has ever been since: in fact, the distribution at that time is much more like that shown in the Domesday Book than that given in the 1961 census. The people were thickest on the ground where the soil was most fertile (like the corn lands of the south and east), or where rural industries had developed (as in the textile villages of the Cotswolds, Wiltshire, East Anglia, and the West Riding), or where a seaport flourished (like London or Bristol). In fact, the greatest density was to be found on a belt on either side of a line joining these two ports. A traveller moving out of this area northwards, southwards or westwards would have found the countryside scantily populated, as he would have done in the Middle Ages; and he would have also encountered another medieval characteristic: that the typical Englishman was still the yeoman in his fields and not the man in the street. Even in 1801, when London, the 'Great Wen', and lesser carbuncles like Manchester, Leeds and Birmingham were drawing in hordes of workers from the surrounding countryside, 78 per cent of the people of England and Wales still lived in the country. (The fifty-fifty position, even, was not reached till 1851.) In the early part of the century, a foreign traveller remarked in Daniel Defoe's hearing that 'England was not like other countries, but it was all a planted garden'; and though he would undoubtedly have modified his phraseology had he gone round with Cobbett at the end of the century, nevertheless, even then, England was far from being the workshop of the world. The Industrial Revolution had its birth under the Georges, but did not reach its maturity till Victoria's time. Even so, its effect on the distribution of population is already visible on maps based on the 1801 figures. In 1700 the people were still living in the places they had always lived in; in 1800 they were assembling in the areas they now occupy. The 1800 population map is essentially the same as the twentieth-century one, though the shading is not so dark.

Adelphi wharfs and warehouses, London

This re-deployment was effected by people moving from the south and east to the north-west, and from the country into the new industrial towns.   At the start of the Georgian period the towns, with one exception, were small. London, the exception, was already a monster containing over half a million; in other words, about a tenth of the total. It was probably the largest concentration of human beings in Europe, and was fifteen times as big as Bristol and Norwich, its nearest rivals in England. It is no wonder that Defoe called it a 'prodigy of buildings, that nothing in the world does, or ever did, equal except old Rome'. Bristol was probably at the 40,000 mark at the beginning of the century; Manchester about 7,000, and Liverpool about 4,000. Any town over 5,000 was regarded as a 'large town' in those days, and most of them were overgrown villages of a few thousand souls, performing their ancient function as markets for the surrounding countryside. With certain exceptions, towns were not yet centres of industry, and if a town grew it was mainly by trade, and thus the largest towns tended to be the ports. But the growth of these was slowed down, till the turnpikes and canals were constructed in the second half of the century, by the difficulties of supplying them with food and water. Even at the end of the period water was still being sold from carts on the streets of Liverpool at a halfpenny a bucket.

The bad state of the roads isolated the towns one from another. Goods were mostly transported across country (where they could not go by water) by strings of packhorses, 30 or 40 strong, along so-called roads consisting of a narrow paved track in the middle with a soft shoulder on either side. It took a week to travel from London to York. And as coaches and

A wagon

wagons increased in numbers, so the roads went from bad to worse. In bad weather they were impassable, and goods which a town had to import shot up in price. The heavy rains in the spring of 1751 doubled the price of coal in Derby, and raised it in Rugby from 8*d*. to 1*s*. 2*d*. a cwt and in Northampton from 10*d*. to 1*s*. 6*d*. The local communities were therefore as self-sufficient as they could be; and not only economically, but socially, politically and culturally as well—for ideas and knowledge and fashions need transport, as well as food and drink and fuel. Thus the life of the average Englishman was circumscribed by the boundaries of his 'country': his little group of villages depending on the local market town. This area provided him with his bread,

Thames ferries

cheese, meat and ale. It produced the cloth for his back, and the boots for his feet and the roof over his head. Within it he picked up his education and selected his bride. The government for him was not Whitehall but his local Justice of the Peace; and at election time he was more interested in who was going to put up the money for the new corn-exchange than he was in whether England should go to war on, or make an alliance with, Frederick the Great.

The boundaries of these local communities were gradually crumbling under the impact of improved transport and the freer flow of men, and goods and ideas; but while they remained standing they had important consequences. They go some way to explain, for example, the leisurely way in which the new techniques in agriculture and industry were taken up; in fact, for the general conservatism in all walks of life in the first half of the century. They help to explain the nature of the literature in the age of Pope, produced as it was, not for a mass readership, but for a minority of sophisticated aristocrats and their hangers-on in 'the Town'. They help to make more comprehensible the nature of Georgian politics: the lack of national political parties for much of the period, the importance of 'men, not measures' and the prevalence of 'influence'. And they are the reason why in the normal way you had to go to Burton-on-Trent if you wanted a tankard of Bass or Worthington, and had to limit yourself in London to brews like Truman's or Whitbread's.

THE SOCIAL CLASSES

England was thus a confederation of local communities. But horizontal divisions existed as well as vertical ones—in the form of a very complex class structure. At the top were the few really great aristocratic families: what Burke called 'the great oaks that shade a country'. Magnates like the Devonshires, the Newcastles, the Bedfords or the Rockinghams were as wealthy as some Continental sovereigns, and they looked down on the king of England who had been one of these. But they were not cut off socially from the rest of the peerage, and neither were they essentially distinct from the body of the landed gentry. The English aristocracy did not possess exclusive privileges like the French *noblesse*, for example, which set them as a race apart. English society was class-conscious, but not caste-ridden; and so, for nearly every purpose, the peerage and the gentry can be regarded as one class. Within it there was more freedom of movement than anywhere else in Europe: and that is true also of the movement between it and the other classes. The spectacle of aristocrats like the Bedfords going in for speculative building in London, or like the Devonshires coal-mining on their estates, or like the Howards mixing with the middle-class on the boards of trading companies was familiar long before the eighteenth century. The reverse process was even more common:

Duke of Newcastle

6

the tendency of businessmen with a fortune to buy a country estate, and turn themselves, or at least their children, into gentry, and perhaps their grand-children into peers. Defoe's couplet puts the position neatly:

Fate has but little Distinction set Betwixt the Counter and the Coronet.

But the key test of social mobility, of course, is whether the sons and daughters could join hands in marriage across boundaries of class. This was not

Couple by the Thames

at all uncommon, for business deals (like international treaties in those days) were often sealed in this way. There was no reason why a gentleman's son should not marry a City man's daughter, and not necessarily with the tragic consequences of Hogarth's *Marriage-à-la-Mode*; but to keep his daughter in her own class the same gentleman would half ruin himself to provide a suitable portion for her, for it was the male of the species that conferred rank.

This freedom of movement between the classes extended practically right through the social scale. The exceptional diversification of English social classes helped to make this possible. The middle class is a case in point, for nothing is more difficult than to decide which types are covered by the term. The merchants obviously belong. But how do we place that minority of business-men in the City of London, with in-comes as princely as those of the aristocracy and a style of life to match? And into which category comes a gentleman's younger son, who has gone into trade? We ought, clearly, to include the professional men, the doctors and lawyers and churchmen, who were increasing in numbers and rising in status in this period; but they were a miscellaneous group, too, as they were recruited from all directions, from the gentry, the business classes

Family group

and from the lower classes, for this was a good route up the social scale for a poor boy with talents and industry. The lower gentry also present difficulties, for their birth and manner of life link them with the main body of the gentry, but their incomes place them on an economic level with the smaller business-men. And the rural class next lower down, the small farmers, the yeomen of England: they are not to be classed with manual labourers, but then neither are they gentlemen. The working class is equally rich in minutely differentiated grades, from the skilled craftsman in Sheffield, through the Cornish copper-miner, the Manchester weaver, the cowman, the ploughman down to the casual labourer trudging the streets in any city and the squatter on the common in any village.

It is impossible to give a brief account of the complexity of English society which is at all adequate; but its highly variega-

Oyster-seller

ted nature must be stressed, for it was of profound importance. The road from the bottom of the stairs to the top was long, but there were many steps to scramble up, and each one was shallow. No one was far above or far below the next man; and this was quite different from earlier times, and from neigh-bouring states where there were few people between the landlords at the top and the anonymous and featureless peasantry below. To change the image, English

society was effervescent: countless bubbles were rising and falling as the ferment of activity on all sides of life was transforming the country into the first industrial state and the greatest power in the world. Society was seething, but the structure remained steady: it passed the stage of rapid industrialisation, the most profound convulsion that economic man has yet learned to impose on himself, with its political structure undamaged and its institutions intact. By contrast, revolution was overturning the remaining governments of the *Ancien Régime* and has continued to do so ever since.

Knife-grinder

If the minute gradations in society made for the stability of the whole, the steepness of the climb provided the stimulus for the parts; for it was a great distance from the bottom to the top and the rewards were enormous. In the early part of the century, the great magnates were receiving £20,000* a year and more from their estates, while a labourer was lucky if he was making £20. Sir Robert Walpole spent more a year on wigs than he paid to one of his footmen. This gap widened as the economy boomed during the course of the century, and the bitter tale of abject poverty in which thousands dragged out their days will be told in a later chapter. But there is a brighter side to the story. It was a free society, and the sky was the limit; and the enticing prospects open to the enterprising acted like a magnet, electrifying the energies, the inventive talents and the business acumen of men at all levels, without which this miniature nation would never have made its mark in the world. Many of the great leaders of the Industrial Revolution rose

* Multiply by 10 for an approximate modern sterling equivalent, or by 30 to get dollars.

9

Sunderland iron bridge

from humble stations. Robert Peel the elder was a yeoman who printed cotton cloth in his own house, Richard Arkwright was a barber, Peter Stubbs an innkeeper.

Besides acting as an incentive, this top-heavy distribution of wealth produced a further dividend: the capital for the manifold activities of the period. Had incomes been equal there would never have been the saving indispensable for enclosing and improving the fields, sinking the mines, constructing the roads, bridges and canals, settling the colonies, building the factories, raising the fine houses, or forming those great collections of fine art purchased in all quarters of Europe. From the economic point of view, the Bridgwater Canal, the Soho Ironworks and Castle Howard represent an (involuntary) abstention from consumption by the lower classes. Though it was not, and could not have been, any consolation to them, their privations were the means to a more abundant life for their descendants; for England now feeds, clothes, houses, educates and entertains 45 million people in a style quite beyond the dreams of the seven or eight million of Georgian times.

GOVERNMENT

The paramount position enjoyed by the aristocracy and gentry in the social and economic life was reflected in the dominating role in politics, which they had fought for and won in the previous century. This is not simply to say that they controlled the government in Whitehall. Their grip was far more all-embracing: they controlled the armed forces, the Church, the civil service and local government, from top to bottom.

However, a proper appreciation of the political activity of the landed classes depends on an understanding of the governmental system of the era, which has many apparent similarities to today's, but which in fact was quite different from it. In the first place, the king was the head of the state, and he ruled as well as reigned. He chose his ministers, and decided on his policies; but by the eighteenth century he could do neither of these things exactly as he liked, for he had to take into account the wishes of Parliament. The crux of the matter is that government is powerless without money and armed forces; and since the revolution of 1688 only Parliament could provide these. Thus the king had to appoint ministers who possessed, or who could acquire, a majority in the House of Commons. A king could turn a blind eye to this requirement and insist on his own favourites, as George II did with Carteret, or George III with Bute; but such a deviation could not last more than a year or so. Equally temporary were ministers that Parliament tried to force down the throat of an unwilling monarch, like the Rockingham administrations or the Fox-North coalition under George III. Stable government could only come from a recognition that there were two centres of political power: the King's Closet and the House of Commons; and the enduring ministries of the eighteenth century all drew their strength from both these sources. The governments of Walpole, Henry Pelham, Lord North and the younger Pitt are good illustrations of this.

Now how did these ministers—Prime Ministers they could be called, though this was a term of abuse at least in the first half of the period—how did they ensure that they had parliamentary support? A modern Prime Minister knows that his measures will go through, for he is at the head of a great party whose discipline ensures that the members troop obediently into the appropriate lobby. But, though the terms 'Whig' and 'Tory' were bandied about all through the century, parties on modern lines did not exist. For one thing, about half the Members of Parliament were independent country gentlemen. They owed their seats to no one but themselves, certainly to no party machine. They had no political ambitions, and could vote on measures as their consciences guided them. For reasons of principle, or of temperament, or of tradition, about half of them tended to support the king's ministers whoever they were, and the remainder voted with the opposition. But no minister could complacently rely on them, for they were not robots. If they turned nasty, they could shake an administration to its

11

foundations; if they all voted with the opposition, a government was doomed, as Walpole was in 1742 and North 40 years later. Their presence in the Commons made parliamentary government unlike anything we know today. It kept the ministers on their toes; and debates were genuine battles over real issues and not foregone conclusions. These parliamentary watchdogs thus fulfilled a valuable function—more like that of today's press and public opinion.

But it is a good thing that every Georgian M.P. did not join their ranks, otherwise stable government would have been impossible. A legislature entirely composed of individuals or small groups renders the executive impotent. Ministers either evade controversial (i.e. important) issues, or they are brought down; and public confidence in both government and Parliament is soon replaced by contempt, as the experience of the French Fourth Republic showed. The English Civil War and the Glorious Revolution gave Parliament ultimate control over the crown. Historians have rightly stressed this—but to the neglect of the equally important necessity of government control over the legislature, which today is provided by party discipline. How did Georgian parliamentary government avoid the French fate if party machines did not then exist? The answer is by the use of 'influence', or 'patronage' or 'corruption'—for which the period has been so roundly condemned. And to see how this operated we must take a look at the other half of the House of Commons.

This consisted of the active politicians, the career men, the men who formed governments and led oppositions. They were organised into little groups, five, 10 or 20 strong, each round some great leader (usually one of the aristocrats) whose orders they took because they owed their seats to him, or because he had given them a job, or because they were related to him or had been at school with him, or simply because they saw eye to eye with him on politics in general. These groups were the 'parties' of the time, the bricks with which governments and oppositions were constructed: the Pelhams, Cobham's 'Cubs', the Prince of Wales' faction, the Bedford Gang, the Rockinghams, the Foxites. There was one larger group which

12

we have not yet mentioned. This was the 'placemen': a body some 100 or 200 strong who voted for the king's government at all times and formed the permanent core of any ministerial majority. These above all have been execrated by later writers, and they were bitterly attacked all through the century by the scribes of the opposition. They were attached to the crown rather than to any

Chairing the member

politician, and were a miscellaneous body of junior ministers, civil servants, army and navy officers, members of the Household, government contractors, sinecure and pension holders, and members of those boroughs, like Harwich and Orford, which the government always had in its pocket. 'Lackeys' they may have been, or 'King's Friends' or 'janissaries'; but they were essential to the stability of parliamentary government.

Thus a Prime Minister formed his majority out of the 'placemen', and the followers of whichever aristocratic leaders had helped him to set up a government. There is no doubt that 'influence' played the major role here; but the system is absolved from the charges of utter baseness which have been hurled at it, by the necessity of placating those guardians of public honour, the independent gentry. Patronage was essential, but by itself was not enough.

We have been talking about 'government boroughs' and seats 'owned' by aristocrats. How was it possible for safe seats to exist before the days of nationally organised parties? To explain this we must briefly examine what went on in the constituencies. First of all, there were about 200 boroughs electing two members each, but the franchise varied from place to place.

13

In some boroughs only members of the corporation voted; in others all the freemen. The widest franchise tended to be in 'scot and lot' boroughs, where the rate-payers voted; and in 'potwalloper' boroughs, where the voters were all those not on poor relief—those who kept their own pot boiling on their own hearth. The narrowest roll was in those boroughs where the vote was attached, not to human beings, but to pieces of property held by a medieval form of land-holding called 'burgage-tenure'. Since votes were cast openly at the hustings, there was room for every kind of pressure by powerful men. Moreover, there was little connection between general elections and the formation of governments. Where there was a connection, it was the opposite way round from today; that is, a new government might hold an election to get the sort of parliament it wanted. Today, the people vote to get the sort of government it wants; in Georgian times the electors were simply choosing M.P.s. That meant that contests were fought on local and personal matters, rather than on great issues of policy put to the electorate by nation-wide party machines.

Electioneering for Georgian candidates, then, demanded its own special techniques. In each borough there were 'interests' to woo or to whip. It might be the corporation, or the weavers, or the freemen, or the Dissenters or the shipbuilders. The Earl of Bristol kept the corporation of Bury St Edmunds up to the mark for many years by regular *douceurs*: a dinner of 29 dishes with toasts to their wives, or £100 to distribute to the poor during a smallpox outbreak, with six dozen of wine for themselves. A candidate at Carlisle became a Brother in the Shoemakers' Company. He gave them two silver candlesticks and a salver, and 10s. a head for drinks, promising that, later on, his regiment would require 700 pairs of shoes and that Carlisle would get the business. Individuals as well as 'interests' had to be carefully nursed, according to their rank. It might be the post of Comptroller of the Customs at Gloucester for the agent of the Gloucestershire Clothiers; or a night at the alehouse for a potwalloper in Taunton. Sometimes the stick was more appropriate than the carrot: employees could be dismissed, tenants ejected, shopkeepers boycotted.

14

In burgage boroughs, where control depended on land rather than people, elections were less complicated, once a patron had bought a majority of the tenements. 'I was unanimously elected by one Elector, to represent this Ancient Borough in Parliament,' wrote Philip Francis from Appleby in Westmorland, adding: 'There was no other Candidate, no Opposition, no Poll demanded, Scrutiny, or petition.' But in any of the other constituencies, if the electorate was large (say, two or three thousand) then corruption would not work by itself; and speechmaking, manifesto-writing and other modern devices had to be employed. Contests in Westminster and London became famous for this.

Canvassing

Each county also elected two Members, but here the franchise was the same everywhere. The vote went to all owners of freehold property (land usually, but it could be life-office in church or state) worth 40s. a year. This descended low enough down the social scale to make the electorate too numerous for urban methods. Usually, no contest took place, and the leading 'interests' in a county fixed it between themselves to have one member each. These deals might occur between two great aristocrats, or between an aristocrat and the body of the gentry, or between Whigs and Tories. And normally there was no great difficulty about whipping in the mass of the electorate: tenants, poor relations, employees, clergy, or tradesmen. Occasionally, an election turned sour as it did in the famous Oxfordshire battle of 1754, when the Tory gentry opposed the Whig aristocrats. Such a slip-up would be expensive, to the tune of perhaps £30,000 or £40,000 a side.

BUSINESS

With all its faults, the political structure produced sound government; and turned out to be made-to-measure for rapid economic expansion. Big money, whether landed or mercantile, had enough say in policy-making to ensure that England became a business concern with its eye on profit, instead of a dictator's plaything reaching out for glory. At home, the state held the ring while the business-men got on with the job: abroad, it captured markets for them by armed aggression. It even ensured the necessary austerity in the mass of the people, for paternal government was not to be expected of a gelded monarchy and an unwilling parliament.

The mainspring of the whole economy was agriculture. Cattle and sheep, for example, besides producing meat, supplied the raw materials for a number of industries: wool for the weaver, skins for the tanner, fat for the candle-maker and soap-boiler, horns for the cutler and bones for the glue-manufacturer. But the influence of agriculture went deeper. A bad harvest could depress the whole economy by leaving consumers with nothing to spend on manufactured goods. A good one could have a tonic effect all round.

Georgian agriculture was certainly not stagnant, though many of the improvements associated with the so-called 'Agrarian Revolution' were well advanced before this period opened. It was mainly a question of low prices forcing farmers to cut costs by more intensive production. The use of turnips as a field crop was established in High Suffolk in the 1650s. This revolutionary fodder, along with others such as clover, sainfoin and lucerne, was spreading in the early Georgian period in the light soils of the south and east. And so were marling and manuring to give these soils body. The four-course rotation was thus well past the experimental stage by the time Lord Townshend retired from politics or Coke took over at Holkham. These new techniques, besides improving animal husbandry by providing winter food, did away with fallow and made for greater yields. By using them, the farmers in these old-enclosed areas were able to show a profit in low-price periods when

16

the traditional grain producers on the open clay of the Midlands were going to the wall. The latter, in their turn, began to switch from arable to pasture, and to enclose.

The new methods, invented under harsh market conditions, spread in the piping times after 1750, when various factors pushed up the price of farm produce. The remainder of the land was enclosed by Act of Parliament. The Midlands and the west went in for intensive animal breeding, developing a 'machine' as Bakewell put it, 'the best contrived for converting herbage into money'. In the lighter soils of the north-east they followed the earlier lead of East Anglia. And everywhere the output was mounting. Between the 1730s and the 1790s, the number of cattle and sheep sold at Smithfield went up by about 40 per cent (though their size did not double or treble, as used to be thought). During the second half of the century, the yield per acre of wheat increased by about 30 per cent. The farmers saved the country's life, for without these increases England would have starved during the Napoleonic Wars.

Sound government and thriving agriculture provided the framework within which commerce broke records and industry performed miracles. The ingredients of the Industrial Revolution can be listed; but it is impossible at this stage of our knowledge to say exactly what weight to give each factor, or to explain precisely why England shot ahead of Europe at the end

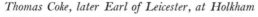

Thomas Coke, later Earl of Leicester, at Holkham

of the century. Foreign conquest, commercial drive, and a growing population (in England and in Europe) gave the stimulus of an expanding market. Capital was there in plenty. The fall of the rate of interest from the seven per cent or eight per cent that governments were paying in 1700 to the three per cent Consols of mid-century is a gauge of this; and an index of its availability. For the growth of such institutions as the Bank of England, the National Debt, and joint-stock companies and the country banks indicated the steady spread of the investing habit.

Another essential feature of industrial expansion was an adequate labour force, which was recruited during the Georgian period from the expanding population, and supplemented by the steady severance from the land of the cottagers and squatters. And to amplify human energy, ancient sources of power were at hand. The water-wheel was turning silk machinery in Derbyshire early in the century; while large London breweries were using about 20 horses each to work their equipment. But fast-flowing streams were not dependable, and a horse cost £40 a year in upkeep—the stipend of a country curate. And so, in the 'eighties, the most cataclysmic of the Georgian inventions, the steam engine, added vast reinforcement to the power of men's muscles.

Again, the basic raw materials—coal and iron—were abundant and fortunately close together. In means of transport, too, England was well endowed by geography. Her island position provided the main highway, the encircling sea; while inland the rivers were navigable and already being deepened and widened in late Stuart times. And the terrain provided no insoluble problems for later improvers on nature: the canal pioneers like Thomas Steers, Henry Berry and James Brindley; and the road engineers like Metcalf, Telford and Macadam.

Ingenious men were plentiful, the most important being the entrepreneurs—the visionaries who co-ordinated all the foregoing factors and put them to work. These were usually thrusting adventurers from the lower rungs of the social ladder, risk-takers with energy and organising ability, who turned into gold what were sometimes the inventions of others. But the captains of industry like Arkwright and Whitbread, Wilkinson and Strutt were just as creative in business-methods as Crompton or Watt in technology; and in those days there was not much distinction between the laboratory, the workshop and the counting-house. The key inventions were not isolated lightning flashes that struck Darby or Kay or Cort out of the

James Watt's 'Old Bess'

blue: they were the logical conclusions to the tinkering and pondering of many other men. Since the scientific revolution of the previous century, the empirical habit of mind was widespread, especially among the products of the Dissenting Academies. Technical advance was in the air, but it required all the other circumstances to precipitate it.

The application of science to industry was thus not a simple process. Neither was it a smooth one. From a distance the Georgian period looks like a century of vast economic advance; but closer inspection reveals that the Industrial Revolution was an affair of fits and starts. Already the ferment was working in late Stuart and early Georgian times; but the 'twenties, 'thirties and 'forties brought a mysterious slowing-down. Capital was twice-shy after the South-Sea Bubble, and labour was short. However, after mid-century, the population began to rise again and production started to mount. In the early 'eighties, all the graphs turned sharply upwards and the Industrial Revolution was off the ground. But these smooth ups and downs should be looked at even more closely. Under the magnifying glass the graphs covering the whole century have a very jagged appearance, telling of bankruptcy and unemployment as well as fortunes and high wages. Wars, harvests and diseases, financial panic and human error were all the time

19

sending spasms through the economy. There were no crusades, pogroms, religious wars or bloody revolutions in Georgian England, but there was enough adventure in the struggle for existence to keep a violent and aggressive people from growing placid.

Further Reading

T. S. Ashton, *The Industrial Revolution*, 1948.
— — *An Economic History of England: the Eighteenth Century*, 1955.
J. D. Chambers, *The Vale of Trent, 1670–1800*, 1957.
E. Hughes, *North Country Life in the Eighteenth Century*, 1952.
A. R. Humphreys, *The Augustan World*, 1954.
P. Mantoux, *The Industrial Revolution in the Eighteenth Century*, 1928.
Dorothy Marshall, *English People in the Eighteenth Century*, 1956.
Sir Lewis Namier, *The Structure of Politics at the Accession of George III* (2nd ed.), 1957.
J. H. Plumb, *England in the Eighteenth Century* (Pelican), 1950.
A. S. Turberville (ed.), *Johnson's England*, 1933.

II

Upper-Class Life

WEALTH

The Georgian period saw the steady accumulation of large estates. Every year the great landed families were adding acre upon acre to their patrimony. Sarah, widow of the great Duke of Marlborough, bought on the average an estate a year after her husband's death. In one year she bought six, in six different counties. It was a new process, beginning in the late seventeenth century and continuing right through our period. Of course, there had been much buying and selling of land for a century or so before; but that had been, in the main, a question of new men, merchants, lawyers and politicians, buying out decaying gentry. In the Georgian period it was different. Though some of the land was bought out of the proceeds of business and government (like that of the Marlboroughs, for example), in the main it went to those who already had plenty. In the previous period, land was the safest form of investment, and a merchant would turn his stocks and shares into ridge and furrow for security's sake: in order, for instance, to leave a sound legacy to his widow and children. The political and economic conditions of the eighteenth century made it perfectly safe for a rich man to leave his money in commerce or buy government stock. Those who bought land had different motives: they were investing in political power and social prestige. In the seventeenth century the land transfers had caused grave social and political dislocation; in the eighteenth they made for stability, since the estates went, not to upstarts, but to the most substantial and conservative section of the population. Thus on the one

21

hand we have civil war, and on the other the 'peace of the Augustans'.

Not that everyone was content, for those who were selling were going through bad times. These, on the whole, were the smaller gentry. Oxfordshire, which had been a county of small squires, was practically monopolised by the Marlboroughs by mid-century. The smaller fry were selling out for a variety of reasons, partly bad luck, and partly bad management. A run of ineligible daughters could put a severe strain on the estate which had to find portions for them. Another disaster could be a dowager with a large jointure surviving her husband for a large number of years. This could happen in the best of families, and was a terrible burden on the son's estate which provided the money. The wife of the third Duke of Leeds survived her husband for 63 years and drew £190,000 from the estate. Straightforward extravagance was a common cause of debt, especially among those gentry who succumbed to the prevailing fashion of rebuilding their houses in the latest style, planting gardens and buying statuary and pictures. A typical debtor was the third Lord Weymouth, who was ruined by drink and cards at the age of 31. But the greatest cause was the land-tax of 4s. in the pound introduced to pay for the wars against Louis XIV. Small gentry, with nothing coming in but their rents, could not survive for long paying a fifth of their income to the government. A second or third income was essential: you had to go into politics (Lord Weymouth recovered that way) or some form of business.

All through the eighteenth century the tide was flowing hard against those who were not in the economic or political swim. There were many like Sir William Chaytor, who in 1700 was seized for debt by the sheriff's bailiffs in his manor house near Darlington in Durham and taken with his servant George to the Fleet prison in London. 'I wish thou hadst seen what a day George and I had yesterday,' he wrote to his wife from prison, 'he mending my old drawers and I mending my old breetches and setting buttons on my ruff coat which was almost worn to pieces in riding up.' Lady Chaytor took lodging in Westminster and died in 1704 having pawned all her belongings. Sir William died in prison in 1721 and the baronetcy became extinct. It is no wonder that such men formed the core of the Country interest, whether they called themselves Whig or Tory, and nursed bitter hatred for the two great centres of power, the Court and the City. We find them opposing Marlborough's war, reading the *Craftsman*, rallying round Pitt and the Patriots, and crying out against standing armies, Continental warfare, septennial parliaments, party politics and placemen. In George III's time they demanded 'Economical Reform', and even toyed with

Squire and Family

Wilkes and Parliamentary Reform, till the general rise in land values at the end of the century pushed them above the bankruptcy line, and the spectre of red revolution rallied them to the establishment.

Many ancient families sounded the sour notes of Squire Western in *Tom Jones*: 'the lords . . . I heate the very name of *themmun*'; but it was different with the squires and nobles whose land-agents and lawyers were waiting to pounce on their property. They have never had such a bountiful century, before or since, particularly the greatest of them. Many of them were families of recent origin, who had done well out of politics and

23

business under the Tudors and Stuarts. The dukes of Bedford, for example, were descended from John Russell whom Henry VIII created Baron Russell and Edward VI Earl of Bedford. Out of the spoils of the monasteries he received the Cistercian Abbeys of Woburn in Bedfordshire and Tavistock in Devon, the Benedictine Abbey of Thorney in the Isle of Ely, and the gardens of a dissolved convent in London, now called Covent Garden. Speculative building on the London property paid handsome dividends; just as it did in the next century on the manors of Bloomsbury and St Giles, which were brought into the family by the wife of the first duke. In 1700, when the second duke succeeded, Luttrell noted in his diary that he was 'the richest peer in England, worth upwards of £30,000 p.a. and in a few years will have £45,000 p.a.' In the eighteenth century the Bedfords began to buy seriously for the first time since their Tudor heyday, and soon no one could compete with them in Bedfordshire. At the end of the century, the sixth duke was still issuing marriage licences from Woburn in lieu of the abbot who had performed this function till the abbey came under Thomas Cromwell's hammer.

Political power was distributed along with the estates. Newcastle shared Nottinghamshire with Lord Middleton, and had influence in the election of one member in Nottingham, Newark and East Retford. He nominated all four members for what he called 'my own two boroughs' of Aldborough and Boroughbridge in Yorkshire. The Marlboroughs had decisive influence over one seat in Oxfordshire, nominated the two

Hanover Square in 1725

members for Woodstock (where Blenheim stands) and after
helping to pay the Oxford Corporation's debt of £5,670 in
1768 they shared the borough for the next thirty years with the
Bertie family. But the completeness of the aristocratic political
command must not be exaggerated. It was strong in the north,
the north Midlands and parts of the east, but in the western
and south-western counties the gentry were in control. And the
Duke of Newcastle, the most assiduous parliamentary manager
of them all, never had more than 12 seats at his disposal, and
he was only really sure of four of those.

The steady accumulation of wealth continued right through
the Georgian period and an estimate of 1783 credits 28 peers
with land over the 100,000 acre mark. Of course, the income
from these vast areas depended on where they were situated.
Owners of London property did very well as the industrial and
commercial areas were developed further and further east, and
the fashionable dwelling houses were built further and further
west. A glance at the London street directory is enough to
indicate the trend: Berkeley Square, Harley Street, Cavendish
Square, Oxford Street, Bedford Square, and so on. The Bedfords'
income from their London property rose from £3,700 a year
in 1732 to £8,000 a year in 1771. And there were many other
ways of increasing the yield of land. The Georgian upper class
is celebrated for the lead it gave in scientific farming, and one of
the most successful, though no pioneer, was Thomas Coke of
Holkham in Norfolk, who doubled the annual rental of his
original estate between 1776, when he took over, and 1816.
Other proprietors exploited the minerals on their estates,
sometimes leasing mines to industrialists, sometimes, like the
Dudleys, working their own. The enterprise of the third Duke of
Bridgwater in digging one of the first canals of the Industrial
Revolution from his collieries at Worsley to his customers in
Manchester is well known.

Yet their enterprise extended far beyond the confines of their
own estates. They had capital in every kind of commercial and
industrial undertaking, and were as much at home in City offices
as they were in West End drawing-rooms. When the fourth
Duke of Bedford imported wall-paper and porcelain from China

25

The Duke of Bridgwater and his canal

to beautify Woburn, he was able to have it carried in his own ships, for the *Tavistock* and the *Streatham* were regulars on the East India run. England may have been a nation of shop-keepers, but the gentry were not a class apart and had no objection to putting their younger sons behind the counter.

Thus the landed classes were not simply passive receivers of rent, and those that were went to the wall. The astonishing buoyancy of the successful ones was dependent on hard-headed exploitation of what they had, combined with further sources of income from outside.

But we have not yet mentioned the most important outside source—perhaps the most decisive element in the accumulation of fortunes in pre-industrial times—and that was public office. The whole range of jobs in the government, the civil service, the armed forces and the Church was a bottomless treasure-chest from which the upper class subsidised themselves and supported their dependants. At the start of the period, the first Duke of Marlborough as Captain-General and Master of the Ordnance (among other things) received £60,000 a year, apart from his percentage of the bread contracts for the army abroad and of the pay of foreign mercenaries, and other per-quisites, emoluments and gifts. Sarah, his wife, as Groom of the Stole, Mistress of the Robes and Comptroller of the Privy Purse, was receiving £5,600; while their two married daugh-ters, Henrietta and Anne, were making £1,000 a year each as Ladies of the Bedchamber. Sir Robert Walpole inherited a modest estate of about £2,000 a year from his father, but a few years in the government enabled him to tear down his father's house, build a palace in its place and live there like a prince. Just how much he made in his 21 years as First Lord of the Treasury it is impossible to calculate: suffice it to say that, in the time of his bankrupt descendants, his pictures were knocked down to Catherine of Russia for £40,000.

Politics at that time was the high road to success in all walks of life, and a wise father got his son into the House of Commons as soon as he became of age, if not before. The House in 1761 contained five Townshends, three Cornwallises, five members of the Manners family (one illegitimate), four Cavendishes, three Walpoles and four Yorkes. Nearly all the leading naval commanders of the Seven Years' War and the War of American Independence were M.P.s: for example, Anson, Byng, Boscawen, Hawke, Hardy, Rodney, Howe, Keppel, Cornwallis, Hood and so on. But the navy was a career open to the talents compared with the army, where the higher ranks were almost monopolised by the younger sons of the great landed magnates. In the American War, Howe, Gage, Clinton and Burgoyne were all younger sons, or sons of younger sons, of aristocrats. The more land you held, the bigger public offices you acquired, and the greater your service to the government, the greater your ability to buy more land.

The stability or enlargement of landed estates, and their longevity, were greatly assisted by the dynastic attitude adopted by their owners, for whom the land and the family were more

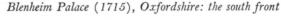

Blenheim Palace (1715), Oxfordshire: the south front

important than the individual holder, just as a kingdom is more important than the individual monarch. Gardens were laid out and trees planted for the enjoyment of grandchildren not yet conceived. The Duke of Marlborough never saw Blenheim as he had planned it, and never, of course, expected to see the estates

Lady and gentleman

which were to be bought for future holders out of the £400,000 he left for the purpose in his will.

But the most impressive manifestations of this attitude are the arrangements made at the marriage of the eldest son of a family. This was the system of strict settlement which became the regular method in the eighteenth century. Lawyers drew up a scheme whereby the heir became in effect only a life-tenant of the estate when he succeeded, and the whole was

28

entailed intact on *his* eldest son. The heir could not sell or mortgage the property except by the very expensive process of a private Act of Parliament. Included in the settlement, usually, were provisions for a jointure for the heir's wife (an annual income) and for portions (lump sums) for the daughters and younger sons when they came of age. These were usually raised by a mortgage on the estate. The system was a very powerful force in holding estates together generation after generation. In fact, it did more: it made for increase, for the wife of the heir brought *her* portion from her father, and this was usually used to buy an estate to add to the main body. Marriages thus became an important method of gaining property. As Sir William Temple put it, 'our marriages are made, just like other common bargains and sales, by the mere consideration of interest or gain, without any of love or esteem, of birth or of beauty itself'.

Marriage to an heiress was a regular way of advancing the family fortunes. The father of Lord North, the prime minister of George III, married three in turn, and the eldest sons of the previous four generations married one each. Many of the heiresses were daughters of middle-class business-men, and it was fortunate that the English landed classes were much less exclusive than their opposite numbers on the Continent. The second Viscount Palmerston, the father of the Victorian Foreign Secretary, married the daughter of a City merchant. The first Viscount married two bourgeois ladies, first, the daughter of the governor of the Bank of England, and, second, the widow of a Lord Mayor of London. The hope was, of course, to marry money *and* social position, and one can appreciate the horror caused by a daughter marrying below her income-bracket as well as her dignity. When the daughter of the Duke of Richmond eloped with Henry Fox, who was a younger son, society was so aghast that Carteret said: 'I thought our fleet or our army were beat, or Mons betrayed into the hands of the French.' The father of the bride need not have been so upset, for his own marriage had been arranged by his father and the Earl of Cadogan to settle a gambling debt, while he was at the university, and his bride still in the nursery. As it happened, they fell in love and lived very happily together.

THE ESTATES

The lucrative marriage, the political eminence, the company dividends and broad acres were symbolised by the country seat. All the leaders of fashion in the Georgian period were building, or knocking down and rebuilding. Their diaries and letters, account-books and talk were all full of it. They went up to London for the Season, for Parliament and business, but as soon as June came round they were off to their estates where their real pleasure lay. Those, like Lord Hervey, who preferred the Town were exceptional. 'I cannot persuade myself to leave this town', he wrote to Henry Fox at the end of May, 1727, 'whilst any body will stay in it with me; which I fear will not be longer than this week.' The following year in the middle of June he wrote to Henry's brother, Stephen, who was down in Somerset: 'You are by this time at Redlynch, and finding your park wall advanced, the foundation of your new building laid, your slopes improving, your puddles filling, and your planta-

Houghton Hall (1722), *Norfolk: the entrance front*

tions thriving.' The magnates aimed at size and grandeur. Blenheim, for example, was designed to rival Versailles itself, and no expense was spared. Vanbrugh and Hawksmoor were the architects, Grinling Gibbons carved much of the stone, Laguerre did the frescoes, Thornhill painted the ceilings and Rysbrack did some of the statuary. By 1710, £134,000 had been spent and it was not half finished. Marlborough, however, was falling from power and work had stopped. Shortly after the Tories had taken over, Harley, the head of the new government, allowed £7,000 from the Treasury to put some sort of roof over what had been built to preserve it from ruin. It was not till the political climate had changed again in 1714 that the vast works could recommence. Shortly after this Colen Campbell began work on Houghton for Sir Robert Walpole, creating a fitting symbol of the prime minister's wealth and power. 'There is a garden of 23 acres to one side of the house,' wrote Lord Hervey, 'and to the other three, the park comes close up without any interruption. The house itself is 164 foot in front. There are two ranges of offices of 100 foot square, joined to the house by two colonnades of 68 foot each, which makes the front of the whole from out to out just 500 feet.' Describing the 'base or rustic story', he said, 'The whole is dedicated to fox-hunters, hospitality, noise, dirt and business. The next is the floor of taste, expense, state and parade.' The garden was created by Bridgman. To do the thing properly, the village had to be demolished and shifted further away. After ten years of work had gone into it, Hervey was able to tell the Prince of Wales in 1731, 'He has already, by the force of manuring and planting, so changed the face of the country, that his park is a pleasant fertile island of his own creation in the middle of a naked sea of land.'

In the middle years of the century, the Oxfords rebuilt Welbeck, and the Bedfords Woburn. In the latter, the Georgian palace was built round the Stuart core. An outside water-closet was installed for the fourth Duke's own use; and inside were two fixed baths, one hot and one cold, the latter like a small swimming-pool. Cipriani painted the library ceiling, while Rysbrack made the chimney-piece in the drawing-room. The total cost of reconstructing Woburn between 1747 and 1763 was £84,970 6s. 8d. The second Viscount Palmerston (whose income was only £7,000 a year till his mother died) could not afford such lavish splendour or such basic reconstruction. He 'Georgianised' his Elizabethan mansion at Broadlands by adding a façade and portico. Nevertheless, he spent £33,000 with 'Capability' Brown and Henry Holland on this and his Town house in Hanover Square.

And the fabric and the landscape were only the beginning.

Heveningham Hall, Suffolk: the gallery

Palmerston bought 300 old masters in his lifetime at a cost of £8,000. Chandos at Canons specialised in exotic fruits, animals and birds from all over the world. Marlborough was picking up pictures, statues and fabrics all over Europe in the intervals between fighting the French and holding his alliance together. He had tapestries woven in Brussels to depict his victories. After capturing Tournai he took down the marble bust of Louis XIV from over the gateway and placed it on the roof at Blenheim, where it still remains. His successor, the

32

fifth Duke, ruined himself with the collector's mania—perhaps as common a cause of bankruptcy as gambling itself at that time.

Entertaining was equally prodigal. Chandos kept an orchestra of 27 players, which cost him £1,000 a year in wages, apart from board and lodging. According to Sir Thomas Robinson, it cost £15 a night in candles to illuminate Houghton. Here, as in most palaces, the feasting had a political purpose behind it. 'Our company at Houghton', wrote Hervey to the Prince of Wales in 1731, 'swelled at last into so numerous a body that we used to sit down to dinner a little snug party of about thirty odd, up to the chin in beef, venison, geese, turkeys, etc.; and generally over the chin in claret, strong beer and punch. We had Lords spiritual and temporal, besides commoners, parsons and freeholders innumerable. In public we drank loyal healths, talked of the times and cultivated popularity; in private we drew plans and cultivated the country.' In 1789, when Lord Fitzwilliam received the Prince Regent, he threw open the gates of Wentworth and entertained 20,000 of the local population.

The hordes of guests are one reason for the size of these palaces. The long retinues of servants are another. But the chief reason was the same as Louis XIV's motive in creating Versailles: ostentation. The object was to demonstrate to tenants, neighbours, friends and rivals one's wealth, social eminence and political power.

These country seats and town houses, with their furniture and hangings, their pictures, statues and books, their trees and flowers, are vivid evidence of the

Sir Lawrence Dundas and his grandson

Children playing

knowledge and taste of the Georgian landed classes. Good taste was widespread. Elegance had become second nature, whether it was in the decoration of a ducal coach or the design of a shop-window in a country town. The early factories, even, were not 'dark, satanic mills'.

EDUCATION

All this is surprising in view of the haphazard and disorganised nature of upper-class education. Many continued to be brought up at home under the direction of tutors, for most of the schools were inadequate. Others, however, were sending their sons to one of the handful of schools that were emerging into prominence at that time, and this was normal practice at the end of the period. For this was the time that the English public schools took shape. As a rule they had been founded, along with the rest of the grammar schools, to prepare the local poor men's sons for the university; but some of the headmasters discovered that their foundation charters allowed them (or did not forbid them) to take in fee-paying pupils to supplement their meagre salaries. Harrow's rise in this period is typical of those schools which made a success of this business venture. Already by 1718 it had 104 fee-payers to 40 free scholars. This was due to skilful lobbying by its Old Etonian headmaster, Thomas Brian, one of whose feats was to pull in the Duke of Chandos on to the governing body. A school is at the mercy of its head, of course, and Harrow's numbers fell very low under the next head who drank and eventually absconded. The next one, Thomas Thackery, another Old Etonian, temporarily built up the numbers again. He attracted the nobility by giving them special privileges; but he grew lax, and when he resigned in 1760 the numbers were down to 80, and the sixth form was notorious for its drinking and gambling. The next head, Sumner (yet another Old Etonian), brought the numbers up to 230 by eleven years of thorough-going reform. His most important measure—and this typifies a key development in the period—was to bring the boarders into houses under the control of the school, instead of letting them run wild in the lodgings they had previously taken in the locality. The school thereafter prospered, though not without a serious three-day riot in 1771, when the boys objected to having yet another Old Etonian in command. However, in 1803 there were 350 pupils, including five future prime ministers.

Thus the public schools flowered and withered, battled into fashion or spent the century sound asleep—just like all the other institutions of that heyday of private enterprise, unpredictable, uncontrolled, uninspected and dependent entirely on the hazards of individual initiative. Most of the grammar schools, as Lord Chief Justice Kenyon described them in 1795, were 'empty walls without scholars, and everything neglected but the receipt of salaries'. Those schools that thrived (and Eton, Westminster, Winchester, Harrow and Rugby were notable) did so by developing certain devices that we have noticed at Harrow. First, the fee-paying element was expanded—like the Oppidans at Eton. Secondly, the nobility were attracted. In the early part of the century, Westminster prospered under Whig patronage; later this custom was transferred to Harrow. It was not a question of noble boys being battered into shape to fit the needs of the school, but of education adjusting itself to suit the young gentlemen arriving with their money, their tutors, their servants and aristocratic ways. When the fifth Duke of Hamilton went to Winchester at the age of 13, he was placed at the head of the school on account of his rank. Eton only placed peers at the top of their forms. The poor scholars took second place, and in some schools that element was squeezed out altogether.

A third measure was to improve discipline by the introduction of boarding-houses, praepostors, fagging and so on; but very few dents were made in the wild animal spirits and thick-skinned self-confidence of boys who treated their headmaster rather as their fathers treated the king. The masters were too few to have much effect on pupils who were doing the school a favour simply by being there. The boys were left to organise themselves, and the result was often the kind of mob-rule that emerges in the early days of a successful revolution. When George III met an Eton boy, he used to ask, 'Have you had a rebellion lately, eh, eh?' Periods of anarchy alternated with bouts of terrorism. At one stage, boys might, like the future prime minister Melbourne at Eton, go off for a week's racing at Ascot; at another they might be mercilessly whipped on their bare buttocks. Dr Parr of Harrow boasted that he never flogged a boy twice in the same lesson. But sensitive boys probably suffered less physical and mental torture from their masters than from their bullying fellow-pupils. The third Lord Holland, when he was a fag, had to make toast by holding the bread in his fingers, and according to Samuel Rogers his hands retained a withered appearance for the rest of his life.

The fourth aspect in which some schools improved was the curriculum. Most schools provided little more than a continuous diet of Latin. Other subjects were regarded as 'extras', which the boys paid for and studied in their spare time. Dr Thomas James, the Old Etonian who put Rugby on the map, wrote: 'Saturday is a half-holiday, and of course (like other half-holidays) is for writing, dancing, French, drawing, or even fencing—as it is now taught at Rugby.' Cowper, at Westminster between 1741 and 1749, read some of Milton and the whole of Homer in Greek on his own initiative. Charles James Fox was another voracious reader who filled the gaps in the school time-table for his own pleasure. He, like many of the boys, had his own tutor with him. This was the Rev. Dr Francis (the father of *Junius*) who, according to Gibbon, an ex-pupil, 'preferred the pleasures of London to the instruction of his pupils'. Fox, however, seems to have suffered no academic harm, at least, and remained a cultivated and scholarly person to the end of his days.

Not that this was any tribute to the Georgian system of instruction, which, though it enabled politicians to quote the classical authors across the floor of the House of Commons, certainly did little to fit them for an era of imperial expansion and rapid industrialisation. The Dissenting Academies, where the middle class learned modern subjects like science, mathematics and geography, were much more in tune with the times; and some of the public schools, like Oundle and

A schoolboys' party

Rugby towards the end of the century, began to attract people by copying their methods. But the remainder plodded on in the old rut.

One department of education which arouses so much public-school enthusiasm today was entirely absent from the Georgian time-table, and that was organised games. The boys were left to their own devices. The younger ones spent their spare time fighting, eating jam-tarts or roaming the countryside. Palmerston at the age of 13 wrote to his mother that he had just acquired a half share in a ferret, and that they were off chasing rabbits. The senior scholars got in some early practice for their adult social life by drinking, gambling and wenching. Cricket was played; and so was the ancient game of football, of course, though Butler, the head of Shrewsbury, thought it only fit for butchers' boys. Private enterprise also organised the first inter-school match between Eton and Westminster in 1796. Eton was defeated, and to add to their chagrin the team was flogged by the head the next day for being absent from school.

When the young gentlemen moved up to Oxford or Cambridge, as many of them did, they had every opportunity to forget what little they had learned at school. The dons seem to have put one half of their effort into writing begging letters to politicians like Newcastle, and the other into extracting the maximum nourishment from the college endowments. Few of them gave any lectures, and few of the undergraduates attended

37

Fellows of Brasenose College, Oxford

if they did. Richard Watson, who became Professor of Chemistry at Cambridge in 1764, 'had never read a syllable on the subject nor seen a single experiment'. Perhaps some of the scholars, sons of artisans and farmers, got down to their books, for they had their careers to make—mainly in the Church. But the upper class lived a life apart. At Cambridge they ranked as Noblemen, Fellow Commoners or Pensioners; at Oxford as Noblemen, Gentleman Commoners or Commoners. They were marked off by such privileges as their admission to the dons' High Table, Common Room and cellar, and by their highly coloured academic dress. 'Our life was an imitation of high life in London', wrote the first Lord Malmesbury, looking back on his Oxford days. 'Luckily drinking was not the fashion; but what we did drink was claret, and we had our regular round of evening card-parties, to the great annoyance of our finances.'

Certainly, little pressure to work was brought to bear on them, either by the college heads or by the tutors their fathers sent up with them. In the middle of his residence at Hertford College, Oxford, Charles James Fox was taken to Paris by his father to round off certain aspects of his education not provided for by English university regulations. While he was away, the head of his college, Dr Newcome, wrote telling him not to worry about hurrying back. 'As to trigonometry, it is a matter of entire indifference to the other geometricians of the college . . . whether they proceed to the other branches of

38

mathematics immediately, or wait a term or two longer. You need not . . . interrupt your amusements . . . we shall stop until we have the pleasure of your company.'

The year or so between the university and the House of Commons was usually filled with the Grand Tour, which became the standard finishing school for the eighteenth-century persons of quality. Not all parents were happy about it. The second Lord Onslow said to Queen Caroline (using the vocabulary to which she was accustomed): 'So, Madam, after I had seen enough of the French to know them and to despise them, I brought my son back again; and thought I would sooner cut my son's throat than leave him to be educated among such a pack of w—— and rogues and fools.' Others felt that the family reputation was safer if their progeny were allowed to let off steam in the masquerades of Paris and the courts of Italy rather than in Covent Garden and St James's Park. But most regarded it as a valuable education. Their children broadened their outlook, practised their French, polished their manners and mixed with the highest society in Europe. Palmerston bagged the two leading Parisian hostesses on the same day, for his diary of 13 September 1773 shows him dining with Madame

The 'Backs' at Cambridge

Geoffrin and supping with Madame du Deffand. On the 28th he was presented to Louis XV at Versailles.

But the chief object was Italy, to see the great collections of Renaissance paintings and antique statues. Many of them went the rounds like coach-parties 'doing' the Louvre today. That was Sir Joshua Reynolds' impression. 'Some Englishmen, while I was in the Vatican', he wrote, 'came there and spent above six hours in writing down whatever the antiquary dictated to them. They scarcely ever looked at the paintings the whole time.' Such young men gained nothing but 'the manners of footmen and grooms' (to quote Chesterfield's view) and some packing-cases of copies of old masters, fragments of classical sculpture (probably forged) and a portrait or two of themselves. The Duchess of Marlborough, while her grandson was on the Tour, wrote: 'As to medals and antiquities, painting and sculpture, I don't look upon that to be the most useful knowledge to anybody, and much less to younger brothers who will have no money to lay out in such things.' The Duke of

Grand Tourists in Florence

Bridgwater, obsessed by his canals, would have agreed with her, for when he died his curios were found still in their packing-cases just as they had been brought from Rome. On the other hand, some tourists were profoundly affected for the rest of their lives. Palmerston was one. 'I never saw a statue worth looking at till I crossed the Alps', he wrote, 'or which gave me the least idea of the powers of the art.' Lord Burlington was another who was deeply stirred: he helped to transform English architecture. In fact, the Grand Tour played a major role in the development of English artistic taste, and the collections still on view in English country houses today are vivid evidence of the effect it wrought.

THE TOWN

When Charles, later third Duke of Marlborough, was on the Tour, his grandmother wrote: 'Tell Charles that I shall choose him of the House of Commons for the next Parliament, but that won't oblige him to come into England sooner than is reasonable, but only secure it for him when he has done his travels.' That was the next stage in a gentleman's life, whether he was going to be a career-politician or not. As Horace Walpole somewhat extravagantly put it, 'merit is useless: it is interest alone that can push a man forward. By dint of interest one of my coach-horses might become poet-laureate, and the other, physician to the household.' The headquarters of interest was London, and when the parliamentary session began in the autumn society flocked to the metropolis. There was much more to the London season, in contrast to Continental states, than simply hanging about the Court. In fact, the Hanoverian Court was regarded as a boring duty. Lord Hervey, whose long career in Court office makes him an expert, wrote to Stephen Fox in 1727 saying that he had been 'at Court last night. There was dice, dancing, sweating and stinking in abundance as usual.' The following year he told the same correspondent, 'I am just come from Court, where I saw nothing but blue noses, pale faces, gauze heads and toupets among the younger gentry: lying smiles, forced compliments, careful brows, and made laughs amongst the elders.' The first three Georges were fish

41

out of water, awkward as leaders of English society, apart from being impossible to work with. They even hated one another: Queen Caroline said that her 'dear first-born is the greatest ass, and the greatest liar, and the greatest *canaille*, and the greatest beast, in the whole world, and . . . I most heartily wish he was out of it.' That was Frederick, Prince of Wales, whose 'ludicrous . . . pretended taste for poetry and the arts' Horace Walpole sneered at. 'I recollect none of his ancestors eminent in arms; and that any of the family should have a real taste for letters, or the arts, would be little short of a miracle.' Their ignorance, or obstinacy, or blustering bad-temper was always offending someone. George II forbade the Duchess of Queensberry the Court in 1729. She had been touting for subscriptions for Gay's *Polly* even in the Drawing Room, and the opera (the successor to the *Beggar's Opera*) was anathema to the government. She wrote to the king in a huff: 'The Duchess of Queensberry is surprised and well pleased that the King hath given her so agreeable a command as to stay from Court, where she never came for diversion, but to bestow a great civility on the King and Queen.' The Earl of Egmont summed up the position on the occasion of another bout of rudeness by the same monarch: 'the nobility of England are proud and presently take fire at any slight the Crown casts upon them'. Most people, though, were less independent-minded than Egmont, and found it necessary to continue bowing and scraping.

They also had to kow-tow to the ministers, for, though the king was the fountain of honour and the source of sinecures, it was the cabinet who usually bullied him into distributing them in accordance with their political programme. Thus society had to dance attendance on heads of departments, wait in their ante-rooms, fawn on their wives or mistresses and drink themselves under the table at their routs. Hervey thus describes what he calls 'the farce of a full Levee' at Sir Robert Walpole's: 'kissing, whispering, bowing, squeezing hands were all acted there as usual by the political pantomimes who officiate at those weekly performances, where several boons are asked which are not so much as promised, and several promised which will never be granted'.

Though politics was the prime lever of their actions, and their favourite topic of conversation, they had much other business to despatch in their brief, bustling residence in the capital. There were lawyers to see and cases to hear in Westminster Hall; bankers to consult in the City; physicians to call in; architects, hairdressers, wig-makers, tailors and dressmakers to set to work. And every day was a continuous round of social engagements which began before breakfast and ended after supper. Some magnates had great town houses to establish their headquarters in. The Bedfords, for example, decamped from Woburn to Bedford House which occupied the north side of Bloomsbury Square. But few went to these lengths. (This was a London idiosyncrasy which surprised foreigners.) Instead, they bought, or took for the Season, a more modest mansion among the terraces and squares that were being laid out further and further west as the century progressed. At the start of the period Bloomsbury and Soho were fashionable; at the end it was Mayfair. 'Had they not been stopped by the walls of Hyde Park', wrote Fielding, 'it is more than probable they would by this time have arrived at Kensington.'

From these dwellings they sallied forth to pick up the latest news and gossip in the coffee-house or chocolate-house. This

Bloomsbury Square in 1787, with Bedford House

Brooks's

was the communications industry in almost its primitive simplicity, at one remove from the market-place. The desperate shortage of hard information at that time inflated its value to famine heights. Rumour and gossip were appreciated almost as much. Everybody, to use Hervey's phrase, went 'hawking about for news'. They spent hour upon hour in coffee-houses, taverns and clubs giving it and getting it; and when they got home at night they filled their diaries and letters with it. The chief resorts of the quality were the coffee- and chocolate-houses in St James's Street and Pall Mall; and in the second half of the period these evolved into clubs. White's, Boodle's, the Cocoa Tree and Almack's (later known as Brooks's) were all a step from one another in St James's Street. The basic occupation here was gambling, for stakes which rose higher as the years passed. It was the national weakness, from the Court down to the humblest ale-house. Sir Charles Hanbury-Williams described Lord Hervey's early education as follows: 'The beginning of his life was spent in attending his father at Newmarket and his mother at the gaming-table.' At the age of 16, Charles James Fox and his elder brother lost £32,000 in three days' and three nights' play. Brooks's had a rule which read: 'Every person playing at the new Quinze table to keep fifty guineas before him.' And the Betting Book at that club reveals that the wagers extended far beyond cards and dice, to any aspect of life in which chance played a part, such as the fecundity of a duchess, or the longevity of a bishop. According to a story in circulation in the Town in the 1760s, Lord Edgecumbe, acting as a Teller in a House of Commons division, from force of habit began 'calling out the numbers one, two, three, four, five, six, seven, eight, nine, ten, knave, queen, king.'

Lord Carlisle described George Selwyn's life in Town as follows: 'You get up at nine; sit till twelve in your night-gown; creep down to White's, and spend five hours at table; sleep till you can escape your supper reckoning; and then make two wretches carry you in a chair, with three pints of claret in you, three miles for a shilling.' But there was more to London life than that for most people. There was the theatre, the opera, gallantry at Vauxhall or Ranelagh, and more doubtful goings-on at masquerades and *bagnios*. The second Lord Palmerston's precise diary enables us to see how a typical Georgian aristocrat spent every day over a period of 37 years. In February and March, 1765, he dined with the Duchess of Ancaster, the Duchess of Marlborough, the Duchess of Bedford, the Spencers, the Speaker, Lord Portland and David Garrick. His annual summary for the year 1770, after enumerating the houses he went to most, goes on: 'When unengaged I dined much at Almack's Club in Pall Mall, where there was a constant and

The Rotunda at Ranelagh

excellent society. On a Saturday I dined at a club at the St Alban's Tavern, called the Opera Club.'

All this involved a prodigious intake of food and drink. Breakfast was late and light: usually tea and bread and butter. Dinner was at two or three at the start of the century, and at five or later towards the end. Supper was any time between nine and two in the morning. The Duke of Marlborough celebrated the birth of his fourth son with a supper which included roast beef, mutton, pork; loin and fillet of veal; pork and mutton pies; chicken, ducks, geese roasted; boiled tongues, hog's head and two dishes of souse; two plum puddings, and one apple pie. Dinner, the most important meal, was less restrained. When it was over, the ladies would retire and a long bout of toasts would begin, the gentlemen occasionally relieving themselves in a chamber-pot in the sideboard drawer. Drink was another national passion.

'Drunk as a lord' is an eighteenth-century phrase with a sound empirical basis. The leaders of the nation provided the model for the rest: Walpole, Bolingbroke and Carteret, to take one political generation, were Gargantuan topers. The Duke of Newcastle, according to Hervey in 1731, 'was t'other night most excessively drunk, and the next morning fearing he might have said or done something improper to the Princess Royal with whom he had a great deal of conversation, he came to her making a thousand excuses for his conduct, to which she very graciously answered: *"Mon Dieu, vous étiez charmant; vous ne m'avez jamais si bien diverti de votre vie. Je voudrais vous voir toujours ivre".*' When Northington was appointed Lord Chancellor, he persuaded George III to close down the evening sessions of Chancery on Wednesdays and Fridays, so that he could finish his bottle of port after dinner. Gout got him eventually, and in his later years he went by the sobriquet of 'Surly Bob'.

THE COUNTRY

In view of this suicidal diet, it was fortunate that the Season was as good as over by early June, and that everyone (apart from the Herveys and Selwyns) got away to some fresh air and exercise on their estates. Arthur Young noticed the English peculiarity here. 'Banishment alone', he wrote, 'will force the French to execute what the English do from pleasure—reside upon and adorn their estates.' Scarcely a minister would be found in his office at that time of year, and the great issues of policy were decided in bucolic surroundings at Claremont or Stowe or Houghton. At the last, says Hervey, the usual plan was 'to hunt, be noisy, jolly, drunk, comical, and pure merry during the recess'. Slightly lower down the social scale, things were not so very different according to the Rev. Robert Knipe, who told Francis Place that in Cheshire 'in his youth he was intimately acquainted with the principal gentry of the country. . . . Fox-hunting, drinking, bawling out obscene songs and whoring was the common delight of these people.' This account, written in the puritanical nineteenth century, is of course biased. It leaves out, for one thing, all the hard work the landed classes imposed on themselves; for they were never happier than when they were developing their private resources or performing their public services.

Rebuilding their houses and transforming the landscape took up much of their time. Then there was the supervision of the home farm, which provided the household with its corn, eggs, milk, butter and cheese, poultry and game, mutton and beef, pork and bacon, ale or cider. They also spent much of their time riding round to see their tenants, or having them up to the house, to discuss every aspect of farming, for they were knowledgeable agriculturists. As we shall see later, they were the

Fox-hunting

force and inspiration behind the astounding improvements in farming techniques and estate management in which England led the world. In fact, they were at the back of practically any improvement—for the upper classes ran the local government. Since 1688, it counted as a positive virtue on the part of the British government that the state did absolutely nothing for the localities. The nobility and gentry in their various roles as Lords-Lieutenant, Deputy Lieutenants, Sheriffs, and, most important of all, as Justices of the Peace, bore the whole burden of civil and military administration. In the absence of central supervision, there was plenty of room for neglect and abuse. 'I have sometimes thought', wrote Horace Walpole, 'that a 'squire and a vestry were a king and republic in miniature. The vestry is as tyrannic, in its way, as the 'squire in his. Any power necessarily leads to abuses of that power.' But not all Justices were tyrants: some acted as a miniature welfare state. Most were somewhere in between the two extremes, and served the country well.

While they supervised the work of the Constables, the Churchwardens, the Overseers of the Poor and the Surveyors of the Highways in the village vestries, or collaborated with their colleagues at Quarter Sessions, or cracked a bottle or two with them at race-meetings, the landed classes were also preoccupied with the problem of the next election. In a thousand different ways, by bullying or cajoling, bribing or threatening, they had to keep the voters sweet, whether it was their own tenants, to whom a nod was as good as a wink, or some stiffnecked borough-council, for whom a substantial gift like paving

The Parish Vestry

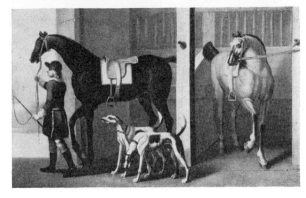

Hunters

the town streets might have to be provided. In between elections, campaigning was a tolerably calm affair—securing promotion for a voter's military cousin here, or a benefice for his clerical brother there—but in election year it was all hands to the pump. This happened every six years or so, and involved either much time or much money. When Palmerston paid £4,200 in 1790 to get in at Newport, Isle of Wight, he absolved himself from a severe personal effort. The electorate consisted of the Mayor, 11 Aldermen and 12 Burgesses. Writing to his wife, he says: 'I arrived at Newport with my companions on Friday at Mr Holmes's house, from whence we were carried to ask the votes of about a dozen shopkeepers who looked as if they thought we might as well have saved ourselves the trouble. The evening concluded with a rubber of whist and a supper of which Mrs Holmes and two other Isle of Wight ladies, tolerably vulgar, did the honours. About eleven on Saturday we were conveyed to the place of the election where the ceremony, which was extremely private, took up about an hour, after which we were advised to take a ride to Carisbrook which we did with great pleasure, [and] returned to a dinner of about 80 people.'

MORALS AND MANNERS

The stiff upper lip had not yet been built into the character of an English gentleman. Men and women were natural, spontaneous and straightforward. They were uninhibited either by inner doubt or outer social pressures. There was something Latin about them, and it is not surprising that they gravitated so readily to the shores of the Mediterranean and filled their houses with the products of its civilisations. When Fox and Burke finally broke their political union and private friendship they wept on the floor of the House of Commons. Men acted on

49

impulse. A slight produced a blaze of anger, a sound thrashing, a duel or a blistering lampoon in language which would have shocked the Billingsgate of the nineteenth century. Frankness was all; there was no mincing of words, no stabbing in the back. The great Duke of Marlborough's widow, Sarah, grew into a sour old termagant, variously known in the Town as 'Her Graceless', or 'old Mount Aetna' or the 'Beldam of Bedlam'. When she learned that her grandson (later the third Duke) intended to marry Elizabeth Trevor, she was beside herself with rage, for Lord Trevor, the girl's grandfather was her mortal enemy. He had been one of the 12 peers created to pass the Treaty of Utrecht which betrayed all that her husband had fought for. According to Hervey, 'she proceeded to call the young lady's father a madman, her mother a fool, her grandfather a rogue, and her grandmother a w——'. The Earl of Pembroke, says Horace Walpole, was 'so blasphemous at tennis, that the primate of Ireland was forced to leave off playing with him'.

And their lack of self-consciousness was not confined to speech. Joseph Farington, looking back, wrote: 'With the apparent show and polish of the former age much brutality was mingled, and great and general licentiousness prevailed in all ranks.' Spontaneity is morally neutral. It can lead to blood-thirsty diversions like prize-fighting, bull-baiting, cock-fighting and Tyburn executions. It produced a harsh system of poor-relief, prisons that were death-traps, a system of criminal law which led Europe in brutality. But it also inspired bouts of private generosity, and bursts of heroism like Wolfe's at Quebec.

Lady gardening

Perhaps the Georgian gentry differ most from their descendants in their attitude to what they called 'gallantry'. It was *de rigueur* to keep a mistress. The Duke of Devonshire had three children by the Duchess, and two by Lady Elizabeth Foster, and the Duchess had one by Lord Grey. They were mostly brought up together in Devonshire House. Little disadvantage attached to illegitimacy. Horace Walpole's brother, Sir Edward, had four bastards by Mrs Clements and they all married well. The Earl of Bellomont seduced the daughter of a tradesman by pretending to marry her, his servant acting the part of parson. Some of them indulged in wenching on what appear to have been medical grounds.

Lady dressing

Lord Carlisle wrote, 'I was afraid I was going to have the gout the other day. I believe I live too chaste: it is not a common fault with me.'

The gentleman regarded the women of the lower classes as his legitimate prey, and the country was alive with illegitimate children. To women of his own class, though, the *beau* behaved differently. There was a rough equality, a fraternal *cameraderie* between the sexes, for women had not yet been reduced, or exalted, to their Victorian position. Georgian ladies had their feet on the ground. Their education was almost the only respect in which they differed from their brothers, consisting as it did of English, a little French, book-keeping, drawing, needle-work, dancing, with perhaps a little music, or Italian. They were mainly taught by their governesses at home, though boarding schools were becoming popular in the second half of the century. Otherwise, they read the same books as the men, talked politics with them on an equal footing, and dressed with a similar finery. Even the ladies' magazines, which were then coming in, had nothing specially feminine about them. The *Ladies' Magazine, or Universal Entertainer*, which began to appear in 1749, included no recipes, no fashion notes, and no household hints. It did contain ribaldry, however, as did masculine magazines. Women held powerful positions in politics, like Queen Caroline or the

Ladies playing cards

Countess of Yarmouth. They owned boroughs, like the Duchess of Marlborough; they electioneered, like Georgiana, Duchess of Devonshire, in the famous Westminster election of 1784. They pulled their weight in literature, had their views on theology, made their contribution to medicine. They hunted and shot, played cricket and rowed. 'They do whatsoever they please', a foreign visitor, Gemelli, observed, 'and do so generally wear the breeches . . . that it is now become a proverb that England is the hell of horses and the paradise of women; and if there were a bridge from the island to the continent, all the women in Europe would run thither.' They lived their lives in a degree of freedom which has only just once again been accorded to them. Thus Fanny Russell writes to her brother in 1743 about an outing she had with Princess Amelia: 'My mistress and her youngest sister, Princess Louisa, went last night to Bartholomew's Fair: did not come home till one this morning and then went and supped at Lady Anne's and stayed there till two. Lady Harriet and Lady Ann went with them, and the Duke of Grafton, Lord Lydford, Gen. Churchill and Mr Will Finch.' In such conditions the frequency of elopements is not surprising, though it is doubtful if they deserved the term. Lord Palmerston did not think so. When Lady Susan Fox-Strangways, daughter of the Earl of Ilchester, ran off with William O'Brien, a handsome Irish actor, he thought the affair was 'contrived by what can scarce be called a stratagem, if we consider the very great liberty which

Lady in coach

young ladies unmarried enjoy in England'. Her parents were socially discomfited rather than morally outraged. 'To remove the disgrace from the eyes of the public', says Horace Walpole, they got the actor a post under the Ordnance in America.

That is not the only example of love overcoming the social barriers. Lady Mary Duncan married a doctor, Lady Caroline Keppel a surgeon, Lady Henrietta Wentworth a footman, and Lady Elizabeth Bertie a dancing-master. In 1756 Shebbeare wrote: 'Men of the highest rank marry women of infamy even, not to say of extreme low birth.' The fifth Earl of Berkeley married the daughter of a butcher and publican. The owner of Berkeley Square and other fat chunks of Mayfair could afford to flout the conventions. We find such easy-going relations with the lower classes in all pursuits. The classes mingled at public school and university. They talked farming and business and ran elections together. They met at fairs, at cock-fights, at Newmarket and Epsom, at Bath and Scarborough and Brighton. When Kent beat All England by 111 runs to 110 in 1746 in the presence of the Prince of Wales and the Duke of Cumberland, Lord John Sackville (later Duke of Dorset) played in the winning eleven under the captaincy of Rumney, the head gardener at Knole.

Such ease of manner was distinctive of the English upper class in Europe at that time, and helps to explain why the crisis of 1780 did not degenerate into a French Revolution. As it was,

Cricket

the nobility and gentry were able to go on enjoying their *douceur de vivre* for a few years longer. Their privileges and pleasures were not snatched from them, but were whittled away by a process much more subtle and far more gradual; and it is time now to consider it.

Further Reading

Brian Connell, *Portrait of a Whig Peer*, 1957.
H. J. Habakkuk, 'England', in A. Goodwin (ed.), *The European Nobility in the Eighteenth Century*, 1953.
R. W. Ketton-Cremer, *Horace Walpole* (2nd ed.), 1946.
A. L. Rowse, *The Early Churchills*, 1956.
—— *The Later Churchills*, 1958.
Romney Sedgwick (ed.), *Lord Hervey's Memoirs*, 1952.
Gladys Scott Thomson, *Family Background*, 1949.

III

Middle-Class Life

BUSINESS MEN

When the Georgian period opened, the merchants were the driving force of the English economy. As Defoe said (biased though he was, of course): 'The Commerce of *England* is an immense and almost incredible Thing.' And the world-wide success of English merchants gives the lie to the fatuous remark of Dr Johnson's to Mrs Thrale. 'Do not be frighted', he said when she was having trouble running her late husband's brewery. 'Trade could not be managed by those who manage it, if it had much difficulty.' Nothing could be further from the truth. The Georgian merchants were not buoyed up on some impersonal tide of economic change: they fought every inch of the way up the graphs which record their achievements.

Some of them fought so successfully that they thrust themselves outside the classes considered here, by becoming gentlemen. The greatest of them belonged to the companies of the City of London. Their agents were importing iron from Sweden, tea from China, and sugar from the West Indies. They bought tobacco in Virginia and sold it in Moscow; and they sold English cloth in the four corners of the earth. They had their irons in every fire: they

Boatman on the Thames

controlled the Bank of England, they victualled the army and navy, they lent money to the government and paid Charles James Fox's gambling debts. Some of them warranted the dithyrambs of Defoe who wrote: '*Our Merchants are Princes, greater and richer, and more powerful than some sovereign Princes.*' Samson Gideon, the Jewish financier, is a good example of the thrust and skill that could pay such dividends in that buoyant society. At the age of twenty he began to speculate in Change Alley and at Garraway's and Jonathan's coffee houses in lottery tickets, government securities and the

South Sea House

stocks of the Bank, the East India Company and the South Sea Company. In the 1730s he was jobbing and broking in English, Dutch and French funds and marine insurance. During the War of Austrian Succession he cracked the hard core of anti-Jewish sentiment in Treasury circles, raised money among his co-religionists to help finance the fighting, and became a most valued adviser to the Pelhams and the Bank of England on all matters of high finance. Each year for 40 years he calculated his capital. It rose from £1,500 in 1719, to £44,650 in 1740, to £180,000 in 1750 and £350,000 in 1759. He married an

56

English Protestant wife, obtained a coat of arms, bought Belvedere House in Kent from Lord Baltimore, and decorated it with some of Sir Robert Walpole's pictures that he bought from Horace. He added various other estates in Buckinghamshire and Lincolnshire, including the Manor of Spalding. In spite of the fact that, as he put it in an application to the government, he had his children 'baptised by the Sub-dean of St. Paul's [a] few days after their birth', the ministers repeatedly refused him a peerage, eventually conferring a baronetcy on his son, a thirteen-year-old pupil at Eton.

But London had no monopoly of tycoons: each of the great provincial ports like Bristol and Liverpool, Newcastle and Hull, had its own coterie of hustling entrepreneurs. At Gateshead on the Tyne, William Cotesworth pulled the strings of a vast medley of trading operations. He began the son of a yeoman and apprentice to a tallow-chandler; he ended as an 'Esquire', of Park Place, Gateshead, having been Mayor, Justice of the Peace and Sheriff of Northumberland. He collected tallow from all over the north of England and sold it throughout the world. He imported indigo, cochineal, logwood, woad and other dyes from the Indies and the Middle East; flax, tow, madder and whale-fins from Rotterdam; alum from Hamburg; wine, cherry-brandy and prunes from Bordeaux; wheat, rye, barley, beans and hops from London. He dealt in tea, sugar, chocolate

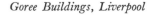

Goree Buildings, Liverpool

and tobacco; and he sold grindstones in Sweden and New England. He ran the English Sword Blade Company with German labour till the gentry took to walking-sticks. He was the biggest coal-mining proprietor in the area, and probably the greatest salt producer in the country. As the government's principal agent in the easily disturbed north, he was in contact with the leading ministers of the day. He reconstructed his home at Park Place in the latest style; and after his death his daughter called in James Gibbs to embellish it further. But whether he belonged to the middle class or the gentry is a question. In 1723 he gave instructions to move the dog-wheel which turned the spit in the kitchen 'on purpose to keep the dog from the fire, the wheel out of the way and the dog prevented from shitting upon anything it could. The dog must shit in the pot.'

Immediately below this level was a stratum of business-men of every kind in every town in the land: country bankers, wholesale dealers, shipowners, shopkeepers and all those other members of the distributing trade supplying the demands of a population growing in size and wealth. It was a layer which thickened as the pace of economic life accelerated, as the towns grew, as tastes became more sophisticated and pockets fuller. Sir Dudley Ryder, the Attorney General who was created Baron Ryder of Harrowby on the day of his death, came from such a family. His father, the son of a Dissenting parson, was a linen-draper, whose shop, at the sign of the Plough and Harrow, was in Cheapside, at the corner of Ironmonger Lane. There Ryder (then a law-student at the Middle Temple) used to repair to buy a suit-length, look over the attractive customers or touch his father for some cash. In June 1715 he got £12 out of him; in the following October another £7. In the following July his father decided to give him an allowance. 'He asked me', says Ryder's Diary, 'what he should allow me, whether £50 a year would not be enough, and after some time said he

Shopkeeper

would allow me £80 per annum, which I thought little enough to provide clothes and everything.' They were a reasonably prosperous family, and possessed a country house at Hackney where they usually spent the week-end, like many another business family. 'The greatest ambition of the London shop-keeper', said *The Idler*, 'is to retire to

Draper's shop

Stratford or to Hackney.' The Ryders' neighbours out there were people like Samuel Powell the grocer, Allard Denn the brewer, Edward Anthony the lawyer and Mr Marsh the solicitor.

PROFESSIONAL MEN

The last two, and Dudley Ryder himself, are representative of another segment of the Georgian middle classes: the professional men. The burgeoning wealth of all classes and the increasing complexity of social and economic relations swelled the ranks of the lawyers, doctors, civil servants, clergy, soldiers, sailors, architects, teachers, writers and actors. At the same time it raised their status. Many of these occupations began the century as trades, and ended it as professions. Architecture became a respectable career whose practitioners were no longer aristocratic hirelings or speculative builders. Again, David Garrick's place in society indicates the long way the actors had come since the days when 'licentious and dissolute manners', as Boswell put it, were typical of that walk of life. 'In our own time', he added, 'such a change has taken place, that there is no longer room for such an unfavourable distinction.'

In the legal profession, the Bar had long been a route to wealth and nobility; but the lower ranks, the attorneys, were regarded at first with disdain, as batteners on the misfortunes of others. Swift called them 'a society of men bred up from their youth in the art of proving, by words multiplied for the purpose, that white is black, and black is white, according as they are paid'. They may have done a lot of dirty work, but the gathering demand for their services by the upper classes was bound to raise them from the mud, particularly when they formed a professional association. It is difficult to think of any pie in which they did not have a finger. The Marquess of Rockingham's vast estates were managed by the Yorkshire attorney, Richard Fenton, who supervised all the conveyancy work, the

Lawyers in Westminster Hall

marriage settlements, the private bills in Parliament, the elections to the House of Commons. Samuel Dawson of Sheffield, like many of his colleagues, dealt in wills, leases, business-partnerships. He handled work for the Cutlers' Company, turnpike trusts and canal proprietors, while manorial business kept him busy with court-rolls, presentments, rents, maps and plans. The county families who ran local government as Lords Lieutenant and Justices of the Peace needed the attorneys

60

as Clerks of the Peace and Town Clerks to guide them through the labyrinths of the law. Some attorneys climbed to the top like Lord Hardwicke and Lord Kenyon. John Robinson ran the general election of 1784 for George III and Pitt. But in general they formed part of the élite in each county town, men of substance and worth. Their social climb was aided by the formation in 1739 of the Society of Gentlemen Practisers in the Courts of Law and Equity, the direct ancestor of the Law Society. This was confined to London attorneys, but similar societies were formed in the provinces: in Bristol, for example, in 1770 and in Yorkshire in 1786. Perhaps the wining-and-dining side of these societies occupied a typically Georgian amount of their time, yet by regulating entry into the profession, supervising training, laying down fees, striking crooked lawyers off the roll and preventing amateurs like schoolmasters from doing legal work in their spare time, they made the lower reaches of the law a career fit for gentlemen. By the end of the century they were usually called 'solicitors'—the word 'attorney' with its unsavoury associations dropping out of use.

Medicine had a similar evolution from trade to profession. In 1745 the surgeons broke away from the barbers to form the Company of Surgeons. After this their training and knowledge vastly improved, thanks mainly to pioneering work in the hospitals, and private schools like the one William and John Hunter founded to study anatomy in Windmill Street. In 1800 they received a charter from the crown as the Royal College of Surgeons. As far as physicians are concerned, there are three groups to consider. Firstly, the Fellows of the Royal College of Physicians, who, like the barristers, had already achieved power and influence when the century began. They had the monopoly of the wealthiest invalids in the metropolis and were earning incomes of several thousand a year. Their numbers were carefully limited (in 1745 there were 52, for example) and entry was confined to graduates of Oxford, Cambridge and Trinity College, Dublin. Next in rank came the second group, the Licentiates. These numbered a score or so. Trained as a rule at Leyden in Holland, or at Edinburgh, they knew more about medicine than the Fellows, and fought a running battle with

61

Family doctor

them to gain full admission to the College. However, they had comfortable practices, and when, for example, they called for subscriptions to bring the College before the courts in 1767, some of them contributed £100, and none gave less than £50.

The high and mighty Fellows and Licentiates were too few and too dear for most of the middle classes, who were doctored by a third group—the apothecaries. Originally members of the Grocers' Company, these were essentially tradesmen who prepared and administered the potions prescribed by the physicians; but in the second half of the seventeenth century they began to attend patients and prescribe drugs themselves. The physicians objected, of course, but the apothecaries got a firm grip on the market during the Great Plague, when the physicians fled to the country, leaving them in possession of the field. When the House of Lords' judgement in Rose's Case in 1703 allowed them to treat patients, but not to charge fees, they circumvented the obstacle by raising the price of their medicines.

Apothecary

By mid-Georgian times, the apothecary was functioning like a modern general practitioner, treating the ordinary, and even serious, cases, and calling in the physician as we should a specialist. Medical knowledge made no spectacular advances, but doctors were already making use of one anodyne which has been fully exploited ever since. 'My Complaints', wrote Colonel Ellison in 1744, 'are what the Modern Physicians term nervous, a cant word the Gentlemen of the Faculty are pleased to make use of when a distemper proves obstinate and does not yield to their medicines.' Even so, the profession of apothecary

was becoming a respectable calling for the sons of prosperous
farmers and tradesmen, and even
gentlemen's sons are found on
the apprenticeship books. By the
end of the period they were well
established, especially when an
Act of 1815 allowed them to
charge fees. Already, in their
turn, they were doing what the
physicians had done a century
before: they were taking corpo-
rate action to keep the chemists
and druggists out of the gold-
mine.

Village parson

The remainder of the professions can be sketched in only
briefly. The armed forces were expanding during the period
and attracting the sons of the middle classes, though wealth
was required for the purchase of commissions, and political
pull was essential for the fatter postings—like the governerships
of the garrison towns. Plymouth was worth £1,000 a year,
Berwick and Hull £600. The Church and the other denominations (which will be treated in a later chapter) could provide a
career open to the talents. And so could the Civil Service;
though in all these institutions the middle classes were usually
confined to the subordinate posts. At the end of the century
the Revenue Departments employed a staff of about 20,000
people. These were scattered all over the country, of course;
while the central establishments in London, which had not yet
acquired that rabbit-like tendency to multiply, were surprisingly
small. In 1745, the Secretary of State's office, which covered
both home and foreign affairs, employed a staff of 26, not counting
a decipherer and an embellisher. During the War of Austrian
Succession, the War Office had 13 clerks and the Admiralty
eight. Shortly after, an empire was won and then lost, with a
similar team at headquarters.

Whether or not the American colonies were lost on the desks
of Whitehall, the civil servants, along with all the other

professional men, formed a sector of the middle classes whose importance is only beginning to be recognised. They occupied the middle ground between the traders and the gentry. They worked with and for both; they recruited from each; they bridged the gap between the two, passing on to each some of the virtues of the other. They kept the gentry's feet on the ground, and taught the shopkeepers what books to read. By a fusion of

Farmer's family

aristocratic honour and middle-class earnestness, they helped to raise the standards of public service to what they became in Victorian times.

FARMERS

Since we are not limiting the term 'middle classes' to those who were bourgeois, we must include the farmers among them; not the peasants scraping a precarious existence out of a few acres, loaded with debt and making ends meet with industrial work, but the substantial yeomen of a 100 or 500 acres, whether freeholders or leaseholders. In general, the Georgian period was good to them, though they had their ups and downs. Much depended on the harvest. The more abundant it was, the more ruinous it could be. A small fluctuation in the size of the crop built up into a wild swing in its price. Gregory King wrote that 'one tenth the defect in harvest may raise the price three tenths'. Three or four years of plenty in succession left the average farmer in debt, and wiped out the small man. The 'thirties and 'forties were such a time. 'Corn was so amazingly cheap in England', wrote Arthur Young, 'that the nation ought never to wish to see such another period.' In Nottinghamshire, the Duke of Kingston's tenants were behind with their rents, and many of his farms were vacant. At Burton, in 1741, arrears of £103 were written off. 'These arrears', says the Duke's account-book, 'are desperate and irrecoverable, the said several persons whole effects being seized on and sold for the Duke's Benefit. . . . Nott. Smith and Carr are run away and Connywell very poor.' The blow was somewhat softened for the farmers by the elasticity of the London gin-market, for the surplus corn was siphoned off into a record spirit output of eight million gallons in 1742. On the other hand, when the harvest was a wash-out, the flush returned to John Bull's cheeks. He prospered in the 'twenties, and all through the second half of the century. The extreme dearth of 1796 tossed £20 million into his lap. From the 'fifties onwards, the farmers enjoyed a crescendo of prosperity. The steady rise in meat and grain prices is reflected in enclosures, new farm-houses and the spread of scientific methods of agriculture. Arthur Young describes the farmer's 'large, roomy, clean kitchen with a rousing wood fire on the hearth, and the ceiling well hung with smoked bacon and hams'. Some

Making cheese

65

farmers put on greater airs, to Young's puritanical horror; but if they had a piano in the parlour, if their wives and daughters left the cheese-making and bacon-smoking to the servants while they chose fine clothes in the local capital—all this filled the pockets of the shopkeepers, and stirred into action the last section of the middle classes we shall consider: the manufacturers.

MANUFACTURERS

The industrialists, whose impact was destined to destroy the Georgian way of life, began the period as a cloud no bigger than a man's hand. Gregory King does not mention them; yet Colquhoun in his calculation of 1803 mentions 25,000 'manufacturers employing labour in all branches'. His figure of 15,000 for merchants shows where the growing point of the middle classes now was. Before the Industrial Revolution, goods were produced by craftsmen like the spinners and weavers of Yorkshire, the nail-makers and button-casters of Warwickshire, the cutlers of Sheffield, the stocking-knitters of Nottingham, and the cabinet-makers of London. These were in too small a way to warrant inclusion in this chapter. Their work was organised, their finance supplied and their goods marketed by merchants. Big business then was commerce. Yet it was not the big men who ventured out into the unknown seas of factory-production. The Georgian captains of industry usually rose from the ranks, or enlisted from outside. But not from the lowest ranks: for hard work and ingenuity were of no avail without capital, whether saved, inherited or borrowed from relations and friends. Samuel Whitbread the elder was the son of a freeholder who paid £300 to apprentice him to a brewer. Six years later, when he set up on his own, he was able to rely on £2,600 he inherited and other sums borrowed from family and friends in Bedfordshire. Jedediah Strutt, the hosiery manufacturer, was the son of a small farmer and maltster in Derbyshire. He was apprenticed to a wheel-wright for a £10 premium, and worked as one in Leicester till an uncle left him the stock of his farm. He thus had something behind him when he started to develop his invention for making ribbed stockings. The rest of his fixed capital was provided, typically, by his brother-in-law, and two

66

other local hosiers—all Dissenters like himself. Strutt, in his turn, along with Samuel Need, another Dissenting hosier, backed Richard Arkwright when he began his machine-spinning venture at Cromford in Derbyshire. Arkwright himself came from a poor family, and had previously been a barber and publican in Bolton in Lancashire. Thomas Ridgway who knew him in those days says: 'He was always thought clever in his peruke making business and very capital in Bleeding & toothdrawing and allowed by all his acquaintance to be a very ingenious man.'

Sir Richard Arkwright

The importance of family and religious connections is well brought out by the history of the Anchor Brewery in its Georgian period. When the third owner, James Child, died in 1696, leaving no son, the manager, Edmund Halsey, took over. He had married one of Child's daughters and she had brought him a partnership as a dowry. He himself died without a son in 1729, and his nephew, Ralph Thrale, became the fifth owner. He was a yeoman's son, and he had to pay off the £30,000 capital cost out of the profits over the first eleven years. He was succeeded by his son Henry, Dr Johnson's friend. When this one died without an heir in 1781, John Perkins took control. He had been manager for 20 years, and only he knew all the secrets of porter-brewing. His capital, £135,000 by now, was provided by three inter-related Quaker bankers: his wife's family, the Bevans, their relatives, the Gurneys, and *their* relatives, the Barclays. Thus Barclay, Perkins and Co. was born.

The first generation of the industrial middle class were thus a motley crew. The Rev. Edmund Cartwright of power-weaving fame was a fellow of Magdalen College, Oxford, and a village parson. Benjamin Huntsman, the steel pioneer, was a clockmaker. The first spinning-mill using water-power was opened in Northampton in 1742 by Edward Cave, the founder of *The*

Josiah Wedgwood

Gentleman's Magazine. The first silk-throwing factory was started at Derby in 1702 by Thomas Cotchett, a barrister. This failed, and the Lombes who bought it and made a success of it were London silk-merchants, sons of a Norwich worsted-weaver. James Brindley, the organising genius of the canal age, was practically illiterate. He never did learn how to spell 'navigation'. Instead of using drawings, he used to stay in bed for a few days visualizing his engineering feats down to the last detail in his head.

Heterogeneous they may have been, but they all possessed certain important characteristics in common. They were hardworking, adventurous, abstemious, ingenious and tough. They were frontiersmen breaking new ground, whether it was in adapting machinery, organising labour or exploiting new markets with new products. Often from Puritan backgrounds, they were hard on their workers, though not so harsh as they have been made out. Josiah Wedgwood wanted 'to make such machines of the men as cannot err'. But, like Brindley who killed himself with over-work, they were equally exacting with themselves. And they had boundless ambition. Richard Arkwright expected to make so much money 'that *he* would pay the national debt'. Wedgwood wrote to his partner in 1775: 'I hope to . . . ASTONISH THE WORLD ALL AT ONCE, for I hate piddleing you know.' Starting from nothing, he died worth £500,000, having achieved his ambition to be 'Vase Maker General to the Universe'. Thomas Lombe was able to provide a portion of £40,000 when one of his daughters married Sir Robert Clifton, and one of £60,000 when the other married the Earl of Lauderdale. His initial investment had thus paid good dividends. It consisted in sending his brother to Leghorn for a couple of years in 1715 to steal from the Italians the secrets of their silk-throwing by machine.

The capital value of Whitbread's Brewery rose from £116,000 in 1762 to £271,000 in 1790. And by the end of the century he had £350,000 invested in landed property. When Arkwright died in 1792, *The Gentleman's Magazine* said he left 'manufactories the income of which is greater than that of most German principalities. . . . His real and personal property is estimated at little short of half a million.' The fact that he was then accommodating Georgiana, Duchess of Devonshire, with a loan of £5,000 to pay gambling debts which she did not wish the Duke to discover symbolises the arrival on the social scene of a new actor—or rather a whole new cast presenting an entirely new repertoire. But the manifold implications of that we shall have to pursue later.

EDUCATION

Samuel Whitbread the elder put his son and heir through Christ Church, Oxford, St John's College, Cambridge, and the Grand Tour. He came back to brewing with the sister of Earl Grey for a wife, and gambling, hunting, politics, rout-giving and picture-buying for hobbies. The subsequent decline of the firm in his time suggests the incompatibility of public-school values and business success. Ralph Thrale sent Henry to Eton and Oxford with £1,000 a year in his pocket. Henry's reckless expansion of the brewery to make it the greatest in London led to crisis after crisis. Mrs Thrale had one miscarriage rushing to Brighton to raise money from friends, and another one settling a dispute with the workmen. The universities were clearly not strong on book-keeping. When Henry Ellison of Gateshead wished to put his boy into banking he was advised by a director of the Royal Exchange Assurance Company that Eton was not a good jumping-off ground. 'He cannot come from thence into a Merchants' Compting house', said the director, 'without being some months at school in London to learn to write and also Accounts.'

Nor were the grammar schools, to which many middle-class parents sent their children, much better, confining themselves as most of them did to Latin and Greek. William Byrd, the landowner from Virginia who was educated in England,

69

received a good grounding in these subjects and Hebrew at Felsted in Essex, but he rounded it off with a short apprenticeship in Holland, and a period at Perry and Lane's in the City to learn business methods. William Cotesworth, the wealthy jack-of-all-trades from the north-east, sent his two boys to Newcastle Royal Grammar School and then to Sedbergh. After this, Robert, the younger, went first to Mr Wright's, a writing master 'at the Hand and Pen in St Mary Axe, near Leadenhall Street', and then to Jacob Lernwoods and Son, a business house in Amsterdam. The elder boy went to Trinity College, Cambridge, and the Middle Temple. Not all grammar schools were out-of-date, and some provided a good beginning for a professional man. One headmaster of Lichfield (Johnson's school) boasted of having flogged seven judges.

Much more suited to the trading classes were the Dissenting Academies, the educational basis of the Industrial Revolution. So successful were they with their new subjects and new methods that they attracted Anglicans as well as Dissenters, and gentlemen as well as merchants. When the famous Warrington Academy (where Dr Priestley taught) was mooted, it was said: 'It is now become a general and just complaint that some public provision is wanted for the education of young gentlemen designed either for the learned professions or for business.'

Hackney School

Schoolroom

Philip Doddridge the hymn-writer ran one at Market Harborough, and later at Northampton. Here were taught shorthand, Greek, Latin, Hebrew, logic, rhetoric, geography, metaphysics, geometry, algebra, trigonometry, conic-sections, celestial-mechanics, mechanics, statics, hydrostatics, optics, pneumatics, astronomy, history and anatomy. French was an extra. Dudley Ryder's accomplishments, reading habits and intellectual interests as revealed in his Diary testify to the soundness of his training in the Academy at Hackney. John Wilkinson, the inspired ironmaster, was schooled at Dr Caleb Rotherham's Academy at Kendal.

Schools and academies are only half the story, and we must not neglect the traditional system of apprenticeship which provided many a middle-class boy with his technical know-how and moral outlook. For it was not confined to the working classes, and premiums of £20, £50 and £100 were paid by middling people to merchants, bankers, apothecaries, attorneys or brewers to give their sons a start in life. These figures steadily rose, and in the 'fifties some London attorneys were demanding £400. In 1755 Robert Ellison was settled with Hagens, the Fenchurch Street bankers, for £600 plus stamp-duty. By the end of the period London merchants were asking £1,000: a fair indication of the economic buoyancy of the times, and the pressure of traders and gentlemen alike to gain the perquisites of a middle-class education.

MORALS AND MANNERS

The Georgian era was 'pudding-time' for the middle classes, but essentially they did not come into their own in this century.

71

'*Tight lacing*'

Until the last decades they were content to remain political and economic appendages of the nobility and gentry, and their social habits and attitudes were coloured by this basic fact. Grocers sent their daughters to boarding-school, farmers' wives strove to keep abreast of the fashions of the Town, attorneys kept as near as their stomachs would allow to the steadily retarded hour of dining. 'The merchant', says Soame Jenyns in 1767, '. . . vies all the while with the first of our nobility, in his houses, table, furniture, and equipage: the shop-keeper, who used to be well contented with one dish of meat, one fire, and one maid, has now two or three times as many of each; his wife has her tea, her card-parties, and her dressing-room, and his 'prentice has climbed from the kitchen-fire to the front-boxes at the playhouse.' 'As much ceremony is found in the assembly of a country grocer's wife', says another writer in 1772, 'as in that of a countess.'

Even the manufacturers were not immune. When Richard Arkwright rode into Derby in the role of High Sheriff of Derbyshire in March, 1787, there was plenty of pomp-and-circumstance. He was presenting a Loyal Address on the occasion of George III's escape from assassination, and, according to the *Manchester Mercury*, he was 'accompanied by a number of gentlemen, etc., on horseback, his javelin men thirty in number, exclusive of bailiffs, dressed in the richest liveries ever seen there on such an occasion. They all rode on black horses. The trumpeters were mounted on grey horses, and elegantly dressed in scarlet and gold.' It is no wonder he received a knighthood on the occasion. Another industrial magnate, John Wilkinson, was as steeped in upper-class manners as any blade. He kept mistresses while his second wife was still living, and had illegitimate children in his seventies. Even the more humble Jedediah Strutt dearly loved a lord. When he was on a business-trip once in London he sent home to his son Billy a copy of Lord Chesterfield's *Letters*, marking a number of passages for his special attention. 'It is almost as necessary to learn a genteel behaviour, & polite manner', he wrote, 'as it is to learn to speak, or read, or write.'

Dr Johnson ruled that the *Letters* 'inculcated the morals of a strumpet and the manners of a dancing-master', but Strutt, who founded a business which still flourishes today, had a keen nose for a business proposition. His reasons for giving his son a course of Chesterfield are significant. 'You are not to be a Nobleman nor prime minister', he told his son, 'but you may possibly be a Tradesman of some emminence & as such you will necessarily have connections with Mankind & the World, and that will make it absolutely necessary to know them both; & you may be assured if you add to the little learning & improvement you have hitherto had, the Manners, the Air, the genteel address, & polite behaviour of a gentleman, you will abundantly find your acct in it in all & every transaction of your future life—when you come to do business in the World.' For upper-class custom was vital to the manufacturers, not only for itself, but also for the prestige it brought. Georgian entrepreneurs bought country seats and toadied to countesses for the same reasons that modern firms build impressive office blocks or put Shakespeare on television. The first target at which Wedgwood aimed his streamlined sales organisation was the Royal Family and the aristocracy; and having scored a direct hit he wrote: 'The Great People have had these Vases in their Palaces long enough for them to be seen and admired by the Middling Class of People, which

A conversation

class we know are vastly, I had almost said, infinitely superior in number to the Great.'

Similarly, every avenue of political advancement was paved by upper-class patronage, and no middle-class aspirant could expect promotion in the Civil Service, the Church, the armed forces or the law, if he was a social outsider. It is thus not surprising that social life among the 'middling class' should be

A life of increasing refinement

an imitation, if not a caricature, of the ways of the *haute-monde*. And the fact that Georgian society was open at the top was another reason. The middle classes did not fence themselves in with a bourgeois ideology while patrician pastures were within reach of an appreciable number.

It was fortunate for Georgian architecture that this was so, for we know only too well what happened when the middle classes formed their own aesthetic taste. In the eighteenth century this class was putting up farm-houses, laying out streets and squares in the West End, embellishing the market-towns, and even building factories, in a style which they picked up from such publications as Kyp and Knyff's *Noblemen's Seats* and James Paine's *Plans, Elevations, and Sections of Gentlemen's Houses.* Good design in furniture and furnishings, china and silver percolated down in the same way. In these surroundings, the middle classes lived a life of increasing refinement. The French traveller, Grosley, noticed this in the habits of London business and professional people in the 'sixties. 'They rise . . . and pass an hour at home, drinking tea with their families; about 10 they go to the coffee-house, where they spend another hour: then they go home, or meet people about business: at two o'clock they go to "Change": in their return they lounge a little longer at the coffee-house, and then dine about four. . . . In summer the remainder of the day is passed either at some of the public walks, or in a country excursion, if they happen to have a villa near London. About ten . . . they go home to bed, after taking a slight repast. In all seasons, the London merchants generally retire to the country on Saturday, and do not return till Monday at "Change-time".'

The provincial towns were not far behind London, particularly in the boom conditions after 1750, when improved transport

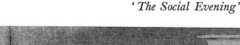

'The Social Evening'

hastened the spread of civilised living. One by one the provincial towns were taking powers by Act of Parliament to light, pave, drain, clean and police their streets; and there is plenty of evidence still standing of the elegance of commercial centres like Bristol, or Newcastle, or Nottingham, before they were swamped by industrial squalor. The amenities of life gradually filtered through from London. Newcastle had its Assembly Rooms in 1736; Liverpool had a subscription library of 100

Brighton Assembly Room

members and 450 volumes by 1758. Manchester built a public baths in 1751, an infirmary in 1752 and a lunatic asylum in 1765. Durham had its first theatre in 1771. The Newcastle Philosophical Society was founded in 1775. And Nottingham's Musical Festival rendered the *Messiah* and *Judas Maccabaeus* in 1772.

And there was plenty of diversion available, especially in London. Dudley Ryder, when a law-student, played the viol and flute, argued the basic problems of mankind at Sue's or

Ninepins

John's Coffee-houses, took the fresh air in St James's Park. He danced at Hampstead Wells, played bowls at Epsom, or mixed with a rougher crowd at Lambeth Wells or Southwark Fair. One summer's day in 1715 he took a trip on the Thames like many another Londoner. 'About 1 o'clock we set out from the Tower, mother, Aunt Lomax, brother and sister, and brother William and Cousin Dudley and myself, in a pair of oars, but it was fitted up in the manner of a pleasure boat with awnings. . . . We got to Woolwich a quarter to 3. Took a little refreshment there and went to the ship which is called *The Royal George*. It has been building two years and half and was designed to be called *The Royal Anne*.' William Byrd, the American, loved Will's Coffee-house in Bow Street near Covent Garden. He usually went there in the early evening to read the news, and then again at about 11—to ring the changes on coffee, milk, jelly, cake and cherry-brandy. One day he went to the prison for vagrants and prostitutes, which was open to the public. 'I went with him to Bridewell', says his Diary, 'to see the people make pins, which was very pretty. Then we saw the ladies beat hemp. Then we went to see the men at fetters.'

Few provincials rose to a sojourn in London. Instead, they made their own pleasure in their own local capital, where cock-fights and Quarter Sessions, race-meetings and general elections

77

passed the time agreeably. In smaller places the more affluent merchants and professional men might mix with the gentry, but Nottingham had two assembly rooms, one called the 'Ladies Assembly', and the other the 'Tradesmen's Assembly'. Similarly at Derby, the Dissenting Strutt and his manufacturing friends of the Unitarian Meeting at Friargate Chapel were cut off from the county families who had houses in the town. As wealth accumulated, traders ventured further afield. A trip to Scarborough might be their Grand Tour; and there they would drink the sea-water as well as immerse themselves in it. One writer of the 'thirties said that 'the tide affects

Race-meeting

the water very much so as to give it a brackish taste'. Another said: 'I think I never saw a more Regular place we have no Gallantry and I think less Drinking so that Bacchus and Venus meet with few customers.' 'Margate', reported Dr Pococke in 1754, 'is a fishing town, and is of late much resorted to by company to drink the sea-water, as well as to bathe; for the latter they have the conveniency of cover'd carriages, at the end of which there is a covering that lets down with hoops, so that people can go down a ladder into the water and are not seen, and those who please may jump in and swim.'

POLITICS

Many of the middle classes enjoyed themselves reluctantly, or at least took their pleasures seriously. A dip in the sea was

Dancing at the Assembly

therapeutic, a ball at the Assembly might produce a contract. Jedediah Strutt wrote to his wife in 1765: 'I was this day thro' Cheapside, the Change &cc and cou'd not help imediately reflecting, that the sole cause of that vast concourse of people, of the Hurry & bustle they were in, & the eagerness that appeard in their countenances, was getting of Money, & whatever some Divines woud teach to the contrary, this is true in fact that it is the main business of the life of Man.'

Prosperous as they were, the Strutts used to let rooms during Derby race-meetings. And it was from a business point of view that the middling people took an interest in politics. We have already noticed that central and local government was the bread and butter of many a barrister and attorney. Merchants and manufacturers were equally involved. Everywhere we find them as Mayors and Aldermen performing the multifarious duties of the Justice of the Peace. As business-men and residents they had a common interest in street-paving and hospital-building, turnpike trusts and Sunday trading, keeping the poor above riot rations and putting down crime. Some had more particular axes to grind. Brewers, for example, could not afford to be indifferent to the local oligarchies when public-houses were licensed annually by the Justices at Brewster Sessions. Some had even bigger fish to fry. Humphrey Parsons, Alderman, Sheriff and Lord Mayor of London, and M.P. for 20 years, obtained a duty-free monopoly of beer-imports into France, it is said, by presenting his horse to Louis XV at a hunting party. Thrale's Brewery supplied the drink at the King's Bench Prison: a valuable appointment in the gift of the Crown.

But the King's government affected every business-man, its foreign and fiscal policies especially. The trading interest, said Sir Robert Walpole, 'resembled a hog whom if you attempt to touch, though you was only to pluck a bristle, he would certainly

79

cry out loud enough to alarm all the neighbours'. He knew what he was talking about, for the merchants got their war with Spain and he was soon winkled out of office. But all the Georgian wars are well known as 'commercial wars'; and the treaties which concluded them contained commercial clauses. The latter usually satisfied some of the merchants and made others squeal. It was impossible to please all the trading interest all the time: witness the row over the Asiento clause in the Treaty of Utrecht, or the controversy caused by the West-Indian sugar-lobby when they talked the government into taking Canada in the Treaty of Paris instead of the French West Indies, which would have been dangerous rivals to English sugar barons. But this is not to say that the middle classes aimed at running the government, for the citadels of power were still fully manned by the upper classes. The business-men contented themselves with giving the ministers a hefty nudge now and then, or sometimes a sharp tap on the nose, whenever a measure especially affected their interests. As large-scale industry grew, the manufacturers, too, began to watch legislation with great interest. The brewers, for example, kept a sharp look-out, for government duties accounted for 20 per cent of the wholesale price of London porter in peace-time, and during the war against Napoleon it reached nearly 50 per cent. It is no wonder that the Borough of Southwark, the headquarters of the industry, was represented in Parliament by a brewer for practically the whole of the eighteenth century.

The other manufacturers formed their own local, regional and even national associations to influence the government, as well as to protect themselves from other menaces like machine-breaking or workmen's combinations. The silk-throwsters of Derbyshire and Nottinghamshire joined together in 1778 to prosecute embezzlers of silk. In 1788 Strutt's accounts show that he paid three guineas to 'the Chamber of Commerce at Nottingham for procuring an Act of Parliament to prevent the destruction of frames'. In 1785, on Wedgwood's suggestion, the General Chamber of Manufacturers was formed of all the important iron, textile, pottery and other interests. It succeeded, among other things, in modifying Pitt's tax-reforms in the

1780s. The manufacturing class was here flexing its muscles, and dropping a strong hint of what it could do if it really began to throw its weight about.

Though the middling people were politically minded, no labels like Whig or Tory, Jacobite or Radical, can be attached to them. They were too varied and unwieldy a group to be filed away so neatly. The voting record of the brewer-M.P.s, for example, reveals that they toed no consistent line, either individually or as a group. They have to be classed as Independents, except for the younger Samuel Whitbread, and he was hardly a member of the middle classes. The merchants' interests differed from the farmers' or manufacturers'; and each group was fissured with its own internal conflicts. The only clear line one can see is the one that separated the pure politicians as well: that between the Ins and the Outs, Court and Country. The general tendency was for big business to be on the Court side. The merchant-princes of the City companies and their brothers in the provinces, who subscribed to government loans, handled government contracts and, having the ear of ministers,

Manchester factory

quietly influenced policy—these were usually to be found in the ministerial lobby. In the opposition sat the smaller business-men of the City and provinces, angry at being thrust outside the magic circle of economic privilege and political influence. They often teamed-up with the country gentry (equally out in the cold) to rant with Bolingbroke, or sign remonstrances dictated by Fox.

REFORMERS

Perhaps these smaller business-men might be termed the 'true' middle class of the eighteenth century, for among them one can trace a certain consistency of attitude. Along with their hatred of the economic and political monopoly in which their social betters luxuriated, they enjoyed a profound disapproval of their manners and morals. We can see their hand in all the voluntary movements of the period which were attempting to instil a sense of shame in dissolute parsons and peers, and a sense of duty in good-for-nothing spinners and weavers. One such organisation, The London Society for the Reformation of Manners, was very lively in the first quarter of the century. Its members acted as a vigilance committee, nagging constables into performing their duties, employing paid informers to report breaches of the law, and bringing delinquents to justice. Each year it published a black-list giving the names of those whose conviction it had secured, along with their crimes. The issue of 1700 mentions 'many notorious cursers, swearers, Sabbath-breakers, and drunkards', besides '843 lewd and scandalous persons . . . as keepers of houses of baudry and disorder, or as whores, night-walkers, etc.'. Between 1692 and 1725, the Society secured 91,899 arrests, and many provincial towns followed its example; but in the 'thirties its energies flagged and the movement drops from view after 1738. It had been impelled by a mixture of motives. Some members were religious enthusiasts, others were snooping busy-bodies. And at the back of many minds were economic considerations. Workers who got drunk not only on Saturday and Sunday but on Monday as well were bad for business. As contemporaries like Swift and Defoe pointed out, these societies tended to concentrate on the poor. 'We do not find the Rich Drunkard carried before My Lord Mayor', wrote the latter, 'nor a Swearing Lewd Merchant.'

A similar outlet for the reforming energies of business-men and their wives was provided by the Society for Promoting Christian Knowledge. It likewise aimed at reducing the incidence of idle apprentices, though by different means. Formed in 1698, the S.P.C.K. was sponsored by the Church of England and enjoyed the support of Queen Anne. Its method of improving the manners and morals of the poor was to teach them to read, so that they could absorb the Scriptures and improving tracts. It issued Bibles and Prayer Books, and pamphlets like 'A Caution against Drunkenness', 'A Persuasion to Serious Observation of the Lord's Day', and 'A Kind Caution to Profane Swearers'. But its main effort was put into the charity schools, which we shall treat in the next chapter.

Reforming zeal withers in the torpid 'thirties, 'forties and 'fifties, though it does not die. There are continuous signs of it all the way from the Puritanism of the previous age to the Victorianism of the next. It was active in the founding of hospitals and workhouses, and dominant in the Methodist and Evangelical movements. In the last quarter of the century it received a shot in the arm from the manufacturing leaders, and showed its stamina in the Sunday Observance Society of 1775, the Proclamation Society of 1789 and the Society for the Suppression of Vice of 1802. It also lent its strength to Jonas Hanway in his crusade on behalf of pauper apprentices; to John Howard in the prison reform movement; to Robert Raikes in the Sunday School experiments; and to William Wilberforce in the anti-slavery campaign.

Exactly what success was

Beating hemp in prison

achieved by this constant hammering away at abuses cannot be calculated, for human happiness is not susceptible of statistical proof. When we consider the gigantic tasks left for the nineteenth and twentieth centuries to perform in the way of civilising political power and humanising social relations, we cannot credit the Georgian philanthropists with miracles. But they made the start—for the late eighteenth century is the 'take-off' period in social reform, after countless centuries of indifference to suffering. Out of the complex chemistry of Georgian times, the spirit of humanitarianism is the most precious deposit, and it was precipitated by the middle classes.

The relentless energy behind this lower middle-class drive to impose its attitudes on upper and lower classes alike—a campaign which has succeeded, perhaps, only too well—was partly generated by the strict code of behaviour they imposed on themselves and their children. We have seen that middle-class education, particularly in the Dissenting Academies, had an intellectual content favourable to business success. Its moral injunctions were likewise appropriate. In sharp contrast to the warm tolerance enjoyed by the scions of the gentry, many middle-class children were faced from a tender age by durance vile. Parents and teachers believed in the inherent wickedness of human nature, and set out to break the child's spirit by rigorous authoritarianism. Flogging on the bare behind was a common punishment for a mild misdemeanour—sometimes ceremoniously preceded by father praying for God's blessing on the thrashing. No time was lost in moulding the mites into shape. 'Oh, how precious a thing it is to hear a little child pray, as soon as, nay sooner than, it can speak plain!' said an educational writer in 1702. Mrs Wesley gave each of her children a day to learn the alphabet at the age of four.

Nursery tales

Henry Longden's father explained to his five-year-olds the omnipresence, omniscience and omnipotence of God; and when they were seven he taught them to subject themselves to their superiors and abhor falsehood. 'After this, he would explain the nature of our moral depravity; our total helplessness, and insufficiency to save ourselves; and the everlasting punishment which is prepared for the wicked. He would then unfold the plan for our recovery and salvation by Jesus Christ.' A proper apprehension of death and hell-fire was instilled in children by taking them to executions, and showing them corpses.

The children thus learnt early in life to imprint on themselves the familiar pattern of Puritan manners. Human impulse was suspect, the pleasures of the body were crushed, dancing, the theatre, laughter, light conversation and leisure were avoided like the plague. Strict with themselves, they turned into harsh fathers and dictatorial husbands—for the equality of the sexes was no part of middle-class philosophy. Similarly, they became demanding employers and censorious neighbours. 'The Lord show mercy to him', said Arthur Young about the loose-living Lord Carrington, 'and by interrupting his prosperity or lowering his health, bring him to repentance.' Any kind of waste made their flesh creep, including waste of time; and one of their most difficult tasks was to induce a proper appreciation of the clock into their workmen. Spending money had its moral dangers; making money was a virtue—though it would be a curious economic system which had the one without the other. If God 'is pleased to make prosper whatever you do', wrote Henry Venn, a founding father of the Evangelical movement, 'your wealth is plainly His Gift, as much as if it came to you by legacy, or inheritance.'

This type of personality, hard-working, thrifty, self-disciplined and gifted at organising others, could hardly fail to do well in a favourable economic climate. And these traits were peculiarly those of the smaller and provincial business-men we have been considering—and thus of many of the manufacturers. The association of this set of beliefs with business success is too well established by the evidence for it to be passed over as a coincidence; but to find a fully satisfactory explanation of it is another question. The exact relationship between Georgian Dissent and industrial advance (part of the wider conundrum of modern history, the connection between Protestantism and capitalism) has long taxed the ingenuity of social theorists. Did business-men become Dissenters because the doctrines of those churches favoured commerce? Or did Dissenters make fortunes because of their peculiar virtues? Or is the explanation at a deeper psychological level: that certain temperamental types lean equally towards business and Dissent?

Some historians have stressed the fact that Dissenters in Georgian England were second-class citizens, cut off by law and custom from the chief prizes in the state, and thus forced to channel their energies into economic enterprise. One authority has stressed the superiority of Dissenting technical education. Another has noted that the probity of Dissenters earned them a good reputation and thus others bought their products confident of the quality, or lent them money in the assurance of their honesty. Furthermore, the Dissenters, a series of minority groups in a hostile world, stuck together, employed fellow-members, married one another and did business together: witness the interlocking Quaker banking families, the Bevans, the Barclays and the Gurneys. And Dissent and business were conjoined in the middle class for another reason. A working man who learned the sober and industrious habits of Non-conformity (say from the Methodist preachers) made money and left the working class. Equally, a middle-class millionaire who gravitated towards high society took on the Latitudinarian colouring of his new associates.

As the Georgian period neared its end, the first of these social jumps became more frequent, while the second became increasingly difficult; and a formidable commando of men accumulated whose religious and moral outlook was totally opposed to the tenets of the rest of society. As these shock-troops of the middle classes grew in numbers, wealth and confidence, they formed their own taste in the arts, produced their own kind of literature and formulated their own political programmes. How the business community ceased to be cultural and political 'yes-men' is not easy to explain.

Earlier in the century, an aspiring merchant or professional man was seduced from his middle-class ways by comparatively easy social ascent. Dudley Ryder's grandfather had been one of the Puritans ejected from his living in 1662 under the Act of Uniformity; but Ryder himself was typical of the later generations of the Old Dissent who were hardly distinguishable from Anglicans in their lack of 'enthusiasm'. True, he was not without misgivings about some of his loose London ways, as the totting of vices and virtues in his diary shows; but he went the

Nonconformist preacher

way of many of his like. He paved the road for a successful career at the Bar and in politics by joining the Church of England. This social transformation usually took two generations, as in the case of the Whitbreads. The contrast between father and son is vividly brought out in their portraits. However, certain developments were reducing the proportion (if not the total number) of middle-class families who could achieve this metamorphosis.

In the prosperous years after 1750, the upper classes had less and less need to sell their properties to Tyneside tallow-chandlers, or concede their daughters to quick-witted attorneys with Sheffield accents. They were in a position to close the ranks, and their grip on power and patronage became more exclusive. This process was helped by the growth in population. The total numbers vastly increased, but the room at the top remained steady. Society in early Georgian times was like a bottle with a wide enough mouth to let an appreciable number through to the upper air. As the years passed the mouth stayed put, but the body bellied into a flask; and the bottle-neck thus produced kept a multitude permanently in their own class. Many, of

87

course, by now (like the converts of the Methodists and Evangelicals) did not wish to adopt upper-class manners. Neither did more moderate men like the Unitarian Jedediah Strutt, who described himself in 1786 as 'having but little pride & no ostentation of my own, not being fond of finery & dress, not thrusting myself into what is calld Genteel Company'. But in any case they had no choice. It was not the rise of the middle class that caused the tensions of the next century: it was their failure to rise. The pressure in the flask was intensified by the expansion of the manufacturing and professional groups: and as all these elements grew rich, confident and class-conscious, social crisis began to threaten. It became a problem of widening the neck or bursting the flask. But this question will have to wait for a later chapter.

Further Reading

T. S. Ashton, *Iron and Steel in the Industrial Revolution* (2nd ed.), 1951.
R. S. Fitton and A. P. Wadsworth, *The Strutts and the Arkwrights*, 1958.
John Carswell, *The South Sea Bubble*, 1960.
Peter Mathias, *The Brewing Industry in England, 1700–1830*, 1959.
A. Raistrick, *Dynasty of Iron Founders: the Darbys and Coalbrookdale*, 1953.
R. Robson, *The Attorney in Eighteenth-Century England*, 1959.

IV

Lower-class Life

YEOMEN

The majority of the working people were rural (whether they were in agriculture or industry), and the typical villager was the yeoman. This term applies strictly to small freeholders, but we shall use it loosely, as they often did, to include leaseholders and copyholders as well: in other words, peasants farming holdings of roughly five to 50 acres. Their fortunes varied from year to year. They were at the mercy of the price-level, which fluctuated according to a number of variables: the harvest, tariff policies, local catastrophes and foreign wars. The same season could be good for a dairyman and bad for a grain farmer. A fall in the price of butcher's meat might ruin a grazier; although if tallow shot up at the same time he would be saved. Moreover, the type of holding created further differences. The freeholder growing for subsistence was insulated from the market compared with the tenant paying an annual rent. For the latter, wrote an expert in 1750, 'to lose a Wheat-Crop is the ready Way to his Ruin, especially if he be a poor Tenant; for on the Golden Grain Crop chiefly depends the Payment of his Rent'. He was in a precarious situation, for a good harvest gave him a low price for his surplus, and a bad harvest left him without one.

What the small farmers needed was a steady plateau of prices, but neither the economic system nor government skill could provide this for them. And if annual fluctuations tossed them helplessly about, the general drift of the tide was also against them all through the century. At the start, Daniel Defoe placed them fifth in the list of seven classes into which he

89

Threshing in a small farm

divided the population: 'the country people, farmers, &c., who fare indifferently'. They came below 'the working trades, who labour hard but feel no want'. Later, in 1767, Arthur Young thought that the small farmer had the same standard of living as the labourer, except that the farmer worked much harder. 'I regard these small occupiers as a set of very miserable men', he wrote. 'They fare extremely hard, work without intermission like a horse—and practise every lesson of diligence and frugality without being able to soften their present lot.' They were ill-equipped for the rough waters of the eighteenth century. For one thing, they worked on too small a scale when the trend was moving away from their kind of husbandry, as a means of feeding a family, to a new kind of agriculture as means of supplying the market. And on the small farm the overheads in labour and equipment were high. Moreover, if the peasants had insufficient capital in reserve to tide them over a bad patch, they also had nothing to spare for the new methods like marling and draining which their heavy-weight competitors were adopting. And, further, land-owners were everywhere reorganising their estates. They were aiming at a small number of large tenants on leases of seven, 14 or 21 years, instead of the medieval hotch-potch of freeholders, copyholders and tenants for a number of lives. Coke and his predecessors and neighbours at Holkham found that this made for more efficient management, easier rent-collecting and higher production. And, finally, this reorganisation was more often than not rounded off with enclosure, by private pressure in the first half of the century, and by Act of Parliament in the second.

This relentless corrosion of the English peasant had profound effects on society, but its operation was too slow and too piecemeal to warrant the term 'agrarian revolution'. It was not, as is sometimes implied, a wholesale massacre by grasping capitalists using the organs of the state. Even enclosure tended to be the recognition of a *fait accompli* rather than a sudden catastrophe. At Wigston in Leicestershire, for example, by 1765 there were only 70 small farmers left. The majority of the land, 70 per cent, was run by 13 bigger men in units of 100 acres and more. And this was just before the village was enclosed by Act of Parliament. And what is more, the small farmers at Wigston survived till the end of the Georgian period. In some parts of the country they actually increased in number after enclosure.

Nevertheless, though the yeomen were not suddenly wiped out, they only managed to hobble along to the end of the century. They received out of the enclosure award a compact holding of perhaps 30 acres; but they began their new mode of life heavily mortgaged. There would be the legal fees of probably £35 to pay, and a further £75 for hedging and ditching. Worse than

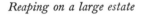

Reaping on a large estate

this, they no longer had the right to graze on the common, and they were thus forced to buy fodder and rent grazing land. With their common-rights went their last mooring to the ancient way of life, and they were adrift in a money economy. It buoyed them up to the end of the century, and then dashed them on the rocks after 1815.

COTTAGERS

Thus enclosure exposed the peasant to the weather, but it was the weather that drowned him. On the other hand, the class next below, the cottagers and squatters, sank immediately. The open-field system had kept them afloat from the earliest times, and in our period there was an appreciable number in every village. At the head were men who owned a freehold cottage and garden, a strip or so in each of the open fields and grazing rights on the waste. In Wigston, for example, a cottager with half an acre in each field could tether one horse or one cow on the common, and graze one sheep in addition. Below this were cottagers with no land, yet even these in Wigston in 1765 possessed about 35 cows and 220 sheep between them. Below these again was a miscellaneous layer of squatters: families crammed into little shacks on the waste, occupying a few square yards of land to which they had no legal title. None of these, cottager or squatter, with land or without land, could earn a living out of their cow or their pig, their cabbage-patch or brace of geese. Many of them appeared on the books of the Overseer of the Poor, and all of them had to find some kind of job.

Milkmaid

They became the cowmen, the hay-makers, the threshers and hedgers of the bigger farmers. But that by itself would not keep a cottager with a family. 'If he has a wife and three or four children to feed', wrote Defoe in 1728, he 'must fare hard and live poorly'. 'But', he added, 'if this man's wife and children can at the same time get employment, if at next door, or at the next village, there

92

lives a clothier or bay maker or
a stuff or drugget weaver ... the
family at home gets as much as
the father abroad.' Though this
exaggerates, there was spinning
and weaving available nearly
everywhere, and a variety of
other industrial occupations,
according to the local specialities.
In Leicestershire and Nottinghamshire stocking-knitting was
the great stand-by. Round
Bedford it was lace. In the village
of Wigston, out of a total of 161
families, there were six tailors
and six shoemakers.

Cottage industry

These families were the chief
sufferers in the changing pattern
of village economy. They had always lived on the brink of des-
titution, but the agrarian changes pushed them over the edge.
With enclosure, the cottager received, perhaps, a one-acre field.
Without the old common rights, this was not a viable concern,
and sooner or later he sold out. The squatter, having no rights,
got nothing. And this was the gradual transformation everywhere: the accumulation year by year of a mass of landless
labourers. Even before enclosure, 70 per cent of Wigston's
population were in this state. In fact, though the numbers had
more than doubled, there were fewer occupiers of land than at the
time of Domesday.

Nevertheless, it is important to note that these labourers were
still living in Wigston. It can hardly be called a 'deserted
village'. In fact, the old picture of the landless proletariat being
sucked into the maws of the factories, leaving their villages in
the sole possession of a few magnates, needs retouching. It is
true that the modern industrial system required the creation of
a class of wage-earners, but in the Georgian period most of these
stayed in the villages, which grew only less slowly than the
towns. After all, the enclosed fields did not marl and manure

Wheelwright

themselves. The new type of agriculture needed more, not fewer, workers, for the labour-saving devices did not reach the countryside till the next century. Neither did the opening of the factories involve the immediate shutdown of domestic work. On the contrary, the Industrial Revolution in our period caused an expansion of cottage production. More and more Wigston workers were hiring stocking-frames, and the villagers of Warwickshire were making more and more nails. What can be said of the country people is that, being severed from the land, they were at the mercy of massive industrial advance when it did come. In the meantime, though, theirs was a miserable lot, as we shall see. They were bruised by the joltings of a runaway economy, degraded by an unwise Poor Law policy, starved by bad harvests and fleeced by war-time inflation.

INDUSTRIAL WORKERS

Leaving on one side the thatchers and masons, wheelwrights and blacksmiths, maltsters and innkeepers, milkmaids and midwives

Iron workers

and a host of other rural workers, we must now turn to those who worked in industry. Here again we find a staggering diversity: from the medieval skilled craftsman employing a few apprentices and journeymen down to the modern wage-earning factory operative, owning nothing but his labour, with all the varieties of the 'domestic system' in between. The last was the most common, especially in the multifarious textile trades. 'In many parts of Yorkshire', wrote Josiah Tucker in 1757, 'the woollen manufacture is carried on by small farmers and freeholders. These people buy some wool, and grow some; their wives and daughters and servants spin it in the long winter nights and at such times when not imployed in their farms and dairies. The master of the family either sells this produce in the yarn market or hath it wove up himself. It is then milled, cleansed, and brought to market, generally to the town of Leeds.' But most textiles were produced under less idyllic and less intimate conditions, by large firms employing workers in their hundreds and thousands. 'In Gloucestershire, Wiltshire, and Somersetshire', writes Tucker, '. . . one person with a great stock and large credit, buys the wool, pays for the spinning, weaving, milling, dyeing, shearing, dressing, etc. That is, he is the master of the whole manufacture from first to last and perhaps imploys a thousand persons under him. This is the clothier whom all the rest are to look upon as their paymaster.'

Weaving

However, he paid his workers by the length of cloth, and they did not regard themselves as wage-slaves, but as small master-men. After all, they were skilled craftsmen, they worked in their own homes, according to their own time-table, finding their own looms, size and candles, and employing their own wives and children as assistants. They looked down on their neighbours, the farm-labourers, but they could scarcely afford to, for the clothier had them in an iron grip. They were usually in his debt, and he could get away with exactions which make a modern factory-owner look like a fairy-godmother. He could slash their rates of pay, make them take truck and force them to buy goods in shops with false weights and measures. Fear

95

Spitalfields silk-weavers

of unemployment made the weavers submit, contenting themselves with embezzling what cloth they could, and occasionally bursting out in bloody riots.

The Spitalfields silk-weavers in the East End of London were in the same boat, and so were the hosiery-knitters of the Midlands. At Strutt's warehouses in Derby, for example, between 200 and 400 workers from the surrounding villages would collect their yarn on a Monday morning and bring it back on the following Saturday afternoon in the form of stockings. A silk-stocking maker could produce four pairs a week, at 2s. 6d. a pair. He made them on his own premises, on a frame which he rented for 1s. a week. Similarly, nail-makers collected their iron in Birmingham and tramped back a week later, perhaps eight or ten miles, with the finished article.

Cutlers

Sometimes, as in the Warrington area, the workman *bought* his iron and *sold* his nails, for all the world like a master craftsman. But his type was rare, and any resemblance between the Georgian 'domestic system' and Merrie England is fleeting. It was much more like the factory system, with workers and machinery scattered over a wide area: though there were important psychological differences, as we shall see.

Of course, there were master craftsmen of the kind imagined

Silversmiths

by those who paint a rosy picture of pre-industrial England. There still are. You would find them in all big towns, in trades demanding a high level of skill, accuracy and care: the luxury trades. Some of the Yorkshire weavers come into this category. So do the Sheffield cutlers and Birmingham tool-makers. But most of them were in London, the most intensely industrialised part of the kingdom. Here you would find coachbuilders and sign-painters, tailors and milliners, jewellers and silversmiths, and the makers of sextants, tele-scopes and surgical instruments. Not all Spitalfields weavers were cogs in a mass-production machine, for the finest work, the velvets, required the attentions of highly trained master-men. The shoemaking business was similar. At the top of the scale was the made-to-measure shop, where the complete shoe was made on the premises. Lower down was the less skilled cobbler, working alone in a garret or cellar, assembling leather cut for him by a leather-cutter. Below him again was the 'translator', refur-bishing second-hand shoes for the poor.

Watchmaker

Watch-making, for which London was famous, was even more diversified. The master-craftsmen were men of accom-plished skill and ingenuity, some of them, like Tompion and Harrison, having a world-wide reputation. But by our period, the manufacture was minutely subdivided, and much of it was put out to men performing repetitive tasks in Clerkenwell garrets. 'The

97

movement-maker', says a writer in 1747, 'forges his wheels and turns them to the just dimensions, sends them to the cutter and has them cut at a trifling expence. He has nothing to do when he takes them from the cutter but to finish them and turn the corners of the teeth. The pinions made of steel are drawn at the mill so that the watchmaker has only to file down the points and fix them to the proper wheels. The springs are made by a tradesman who does nothing else, and the chains by another. . . . After the watchmaker has got home all the . . . parts of which it consists, he gives the whole to the finisher, having first had the brass wheels gilded by the gilder, and adjusts it to the proper time. The watchmaker puts his name on the plate and is esteemed the maker, though he has not made in his shop the smallest wheel belonging to it.' Already 'engines' were speeding up some stages of the work, and it is not surprising to find that watchmaking artisans were prominent in textile machinery later in the century.

We have limited ourselves so far to the craftsmen and domestic workers, the traditional types in English industry; but already there were numerous examples of the sort of workers we are familiar with today: wage-earners working *en masse* on their employer's premises. Coal-mining clearly could not be a domestic craft; and the men who hewed the stone at Portland, mined the copper in Cornwall and the lead in Derbyshire, extracted the salt in Cheshire or quarried the slate in Cumberland all had to go out to work every morning. Nature dictated their place of business. In other cases it was the type of product which brought many workers together in one spot: sail-makers, ship-builders and cannon-founders, for example. Processes requiring special skill, careful supervision or homogeneous treatment also tended to be carried out under one roof, like dyeing and finishing in the textile industry, or the making of army uniforms. Government establishments were the largest

Cannon-makers

of all. The royal arsenal at Chatham impressed Defoe in the 'twenties. 'The building-yards, docks, timber-yard, deal-yard, mast-yard, gun-yard, rope-walks; and all the other yards and places, set apart for the works belonging to the navy', he wrote, 'are like a well-ordered city.' Sometimes it was power that brought about the concentration of labour—long before the Industrial Revolution. By 1721, for example, Thomas Lombe's

Shipbuilding

silk factory was employing several hundred hands, with a 23-foot water-wheel driving 26,000 wheels.

This was a true factory, but whether all the operatives were true workers in the modern sense may be doubted. Even in these large establishments old customs were mingled with the new. In the coal-mines, for example, a skilled hewer (regarded then as the élite of the working class) hired his own assistants. The ancient practice of families working together, instead of father going out to work, lingered everywhere, and survived into the next century. In the iron industry, furnace operators

99

had their wives and children on the job, preparing the ore and picking out bits of iron and charcoal from the cinders. At the forge, the hammerman was under contract for a term of years, and employed his own labourers. In establishments of an earlier origin, like tallow-chandlers' and tanners' works, the men were theoretically journeymen under a master. In newer industries like brewing and sugar-refining, the men were labourers under a foreman. In practice, it was hard to tell the difference.

DOMESTIC SERVANTS

The Georgian workers were clearly far from being a homogeneous social group, and the typical working man that we are familiar with was only just emerging. On the other hand, a species now fast becoming extinct flourished in vast numbers in the eighteenth century—the domestic servants. Anyone not convinced of the diversity of the social structure should examine the ranks and degrees in this set of men. Beginning with the upper servants, and leaving out the land-steward and *maître d'hôtel* as qualifying for middle-class status, we have, in descending order, the clerk of the stables and the clerk of the kitchen, the cook, the confectioner, the baker, the bailiff, the valet, the butler, the gardener and the groom of the chambers.

Domestic servants

Below these came the lower servants, who wore livery: the coachman, the footman, the running footman and the groom, the under-butler and the under-coachman, the park-keeper and the gamekeeper and the porter, the postilion, the yard-boy, the provision-boy, the foot-boy, and, finally, the page. The female hierarchy had a similar pecking-order. The lady's maid (or waiting-woman or tirewoman), the housekeeper and the cook were in the higher echelons. Below them (though not in livery) were lined up the chambermaid, the house-maid, the maid of all work, the laundry

100

maid and the dairy maid. These last four were about level, and right at the end came the scullery maid. Of course, this is the establishment of a wealthy household. A more modest one would begin lower down; but the order of precedence would be strictly maintained, even if the staff (as in a modest parson's house) consisted only of a personal man, a maid of all work and a scullery maid.

Traditionally, retainers belonged to their employers body and soul, and implicit obedience was expected. In Georgian times it was rarely given, for servants were then notoriously insubordinate. Masters had the right to give them a clout now and then, as Swift did when his man was not there to let him into the house one night. When Patrick finally appeared, after ten, 'I went up', Swift tells Stella, 'shut the chamber door, and gave him two or three swinging cuffs on the ear, and I have strained the thumb of my left hand with pulling him, which I did not feel till he was gone.'

Many servants would have looked for another job at that point, and there were various ways of doing this. In the provinces, like some of the mining and agricultural workers, servants were hired annually at the fairs. The American visitor William Byrd noticed this when he was staying in the country in 1718. 'We went to the fair', says his diary, 'where we saw the maids stand in a row to be hired.' But hordes of them preferred London register offices. 'Young men and women in the country', wrote Arthur Young, 'fix their eye on London as the last stage of their hope; they enter into service in the country for little else but to raise money enough to go to London.' Jonas Hanway calculated that they swarmed into the metropolis at the rate of 5,000 a year. Instead of going to register offices, they were often met by an agent or a bawd as they descended from the wagon on their first arrival, like Moll Hackabout in the *Harlot's Progress*. Native Londoners had an unsavoury reputation, and masters preferred country wenches and lads. In fact, an unemployed Londoner would often take the wagon out of town and then come in again in order to get a post. The consequence was a surfeit of flunkeys there. In the 'sixties every thirteenth person you met was one; and a calculation of 1796 puts the ratio at

101

Sawyers

one in four and a half. In 1760 there were 2,000 out of work according to Hanway; in 1796 Colquhoun thought the figure was nearer 10,000. This is surprising in view of the steady howl that came from employers all through the century about the shortage of scullions and maids of all work. The explanation must be that the idle were resting between posts, trying to improve themselves. In any case, in all kinds of work, complaints about lack of jobs, on the one hand, and shortage of hands, on the other, formed a discordant duet all through the middle decades of the century.

LABOURERS

This sketch of yeomen and cottagers, artisans, factory hands and retainers hardly takes us below the surface of lower-class life, but we must limit ourselves to dredging up only a few more samples. There were the chimney-sweeps, the climbing-boys with their black faces and white teeth, scrambling up the flue with brush and scraper, shouting 'All up!' at the top and then twisting down again. There were the sawyers who worked in pairs. They had their distinctions, too, for the under-sawyer got all the dust in his face. There were the builders, the drovers, the scavengers and the odd-job men. And there were plenty of shop-assistants. Some were respectable like Robert Owen in the 'eighties, who opened up Flint and Palmer's in the Borough at eight in the morning, saw the last customer out at 10-30, and got to bed at two in the morning after putting the shop straight. At the lower end of the scale was the chandler's shop, which dealt 'in all things necessary for the kitchen in small quantities', says a writer in 1747. 'He is partly cheese-monger, oilman, grocer, distiller, etc.' The poor got their ha'porths of bread, cheese, beer, coal, soap and candles there; the hawker called in for his breakfast and a tot of gin.

And we must not forget the women, the fish-hawkers and ballad-sellers, the cinder-sifters and rag-pickers. Nor their husbands the sailors, the porters, the coal-heavers and chairmen —Londoners who would come out on the streets at the drop of a tract, as they did in John Wilkes' great days. Then we come to the dregs: the cut-throats and burglars, Fleet-parsons and fences, the gentlemen of the road and the ladies of the street— the under-world of the *Beggar's Opera*. Life was bitter at this level. Like the washer-woman Ann Nichols, who used to arrive at her Hackney employer's at midnight and then scrub through to the end of the next day for a few pence, all these people were only too familiar with over-work, disease, sudden death or a destitute old age; and an existence on and off the Poor Rates.

In a period when the experts advised that low wages were good for trade and that state action was bad for liberty, the lower classes were helpless victims. Dr Deering in the 'thirties described how Nottingham was visited by a 'Distemperature in the Air once in five years which either brings along with it some Epidemic Fever (tho' seldom very mortal) or renders smallpox more dangerous than at other times . . . but in the year 1736 . . . this Distemperature swept away a great number (but mostly Children)'. At the same time, Dr Hillary of Ripon noted the evidence of 'nervous', 'hysteric' and 'putrid' fevers in Yorkshire. 'Many of the little country towns and villages were almost stripped of their poor people', he wrote; and added, 'I observed that very few of the richer people, who used a more generous way of living and were not exposed to the inclemencies of the weather, were seized with any of these diseases at this time.'

THE POOR LAW

Life was short in all the towns, but London was positively murderous. In Bethnal Green, John Wesley found this family in 1777: 'one poor man was just creeping out of his sick bed, to his ragged wife and three little children, who were more than half naked, and the very picture of famine; when one bringing in a loaf of bread, they all ran, seized upon it, and tore it in pieces in an instant'. In Holborn in 1763, a man went over an empty house in Stonecutter Street with a view to buying

103

Overleaf: *Billingsgate market in 1762*

it. In two of the rooms he found three dead women, emaciated and almost naked. In the garret were living two women and a girl, two of them on the verge of starvation. Dr Johnson was told by Saunders Welch the magistrate that malnutrition killed off more than 20 a week. Primitive medicine, insanitary housing, excessive drink, inadequate food and lack of birth control produced a throng of senile invalids, abandoned wives and illegitimate children which overstrained the sketchy welfare services. Add to this the growing population and periodic slumps, and it is not surprising that the Poor Law system was overwhelmed before the end of the century.

The 'Poor Law' is a euphemism for a legal maze whose complexities often foxed the House of Lords and always caused magistrates to reach for their Burn's *Justice of the Peace and Parish Officer*. In this do-it-yourself manual of local government a quarter of the space was devoted to pauperism; but we cannot afford such lengthy treatment here. Briefly, the law provided officials with an excuse not to relieve a pauper till he was in his own parish. You could gain a 'settlement' in a parish in several ways: by being born there (if illegitimate); by having a father settled there (if legitimate and under seven); by marrying a husband there; by working there for one year (if single); by apprenticeship there; by renting a tenement of £10 annual value; by holding a public office; by paying the rates; or by 40 days' residence there, after giving notice in writing. If you were in a place without one of the above qualifications and appeared 'likely to become chargeable' the magistrates would promptly 'remove' you. But let us see, first of all, how a parish treated its own admitted poor.

We will begin with the children—an enormous problem in all large towns, where babies were left exposed on the streets, or their bodies dumped on dung-heaps to save funeral expenses. The retired sea-captain Thomas Coram was so sickened by the sight of these that he worked for 17 years to start the Foundling Hospital; and one of the Governors of this was Jonas Hanway, who began collecting statistics in the 'sixties. Choosing a sample of eleven London parishes (including the best and the worst) he found that, in the year 1763, 291 children had entered the

106

workhouses, not counting those who had been discharged with their mothers during the year. By the end of 1765, 256 of these were dead. But not all parishes put babies in the workhouse. Many of them put them out to nurses at a shilling or two a week. In 1715, a Parliamentary Committee reported 'that a great many poor infants . . . are inhumanly suffered to die by the barbarity of nurses, who are a sort of people void of commiseration or religion, hired by the Church Wardens to take off a burthen from the parish at the easiest rates they can, and these know the manner of doing it effectually'.

The tough ones who survived this treatment were apprenticed at the age of seven till they were 24,* in the case of boys, and 21, in the case of girls. The theory was that the children should learn a trade and become useful citizens; but too often the parish was solely concerned with getting the child off its hands. This it could do by apprenticing it in another parish, thus gaining it a settlement there. The Vestry Minutes of St Pancras in 1722 illustrate the process: 'Ordered, that Mr Batt, Upper Churchwarden, should bind out William Lucas apprentice to what person or business he shall think most proper, and to make as cheap a bargain for putting him out as he can.' The parish funds had to pay a fee to the master (usually about £5), but it was money well spent. As a writer put it in 1738:'if the child serves the first forty days we are rid of him for ever'. The master was on a good thing, too, for he had a useful drudge; and, even if the child ran away, he still had his £5. In fact, many masters ill-treated their charges so that they would run away, for they were only in the game for the money.

Mariner

At its best, the system provided employers with cheap labour; at its worst, it was the equivalent to being sold into slavery. The child belonged to the master till his time was out. If an apprentice got pressed into the navy,

* 21 after 1768.

107

Tailor and apprentices

for example, the master was entitled to all his pay and prize-money. Jonathan Saville, a Methodist preacher of some note in the Halifax area, was apprenticed at the age of seven to a miner. To escape the latter's brutality, he then became bound to a spinner; but his master's daughter was a virago who one day felled him to the ground with a blow, breaking his thigh. He grew up a stunted cripple. To be bound out as a domestic help—to learn the 'art of housewifery'—or as a street milk-seller, or as a pot-boy, or as a baker's beast of burden was bad enough; but acquiring the skills of chimney-sweeping was worse. Here the fees were low. 'Orphans who are in a vagabond state, or the illegitimate children of the poorest kind of people', wrote Hanway in 1785, 'are said to be sold, that is, their service for seven years is disposed of for twenty or thirty shillings.' Masters would sometimes take on as many as 24, send them out to beg in the summer, and hire them out at 6d. a day in the winter. It is no wonder that we hear so much of runaway apprentices at that time. Sometimes they were caught, like Mary Wotton, who absconded at the age of nine, unwisely taking with her 27 guineas belonging to her mistress. She was sentenced to death.

The children were the first group the parish was responsible for. The second was the aged and sick. Here again, it is impossible to generalise. Some parishes provided their rent and an allowance for food. Others billeted them on more affluent parishioners. Others ran a workhouse—perhaps nothing more than a mud hut on the waste. Some parishes paid a doctor to 'physic the poor'; most paid their funeral expenses.

In the towns, as the problem became overwhelming, some parishes provided special institutions and ran them wisely, like Liverpool with its Workhouse, Infirmary, Dispensary and Fever Hospital. But many populous places went no further than a workhouse under a contractor, who was out to make what he could out of it. Overcrowding usually resulted. 'Few persons accustomed to cleanly life', said Hanway, 'can bear the stench of them or stand the survey of such misery.' St Leonard's, Shoreditch, complained to the House of Commons in 1774 that its building was too small. The parish officers, goes the report, 'are obliged to put thirty-nine children . . . into three beds, by which means they contract disorders from each other'. These children were the victims of the seizing up of local government machinery which was occurring everywhere. Tudor institutions set up to run villages could not cope with the massing of population that came in Georgian times.

Apart from the children and the 'impotent poor', the parish authorities had a third task: that of providing work for the 'able-bodied poor'. Their activity in this field was so slipshod that we need say no more about it. We can pass on instead to see what happened to those who became destitute in a place where they had no settlement. Till 1795, the Justices had the power, if anyone looked 'likely to become chargeable to the parish [to quote the Act] to remove and convey such person to such parish where he was last legally settled'. The removing parish had to foot the bill here; but if the other parish was a long way off they could save expenses by dealing with the pauper under a different set of laws altogether—the Vagrancy Laws. Here, the pauper, after whipping and/or imprisonment, was not 'removed' but 'passed': that is, trundled in a cart from one parish boundary to the next till he was home. The costs were borne by each parish through which he was 'passed'. Professional beggars, like some of the Irish returning home after the London hay-making season, found it a convenient mode of transport. A single man, if he was fit, was usually left undisturbed by the authorities, and in a big city parish they would not even know he was there. But let a family arrive in a country parish, or a widow with children, and they were immediately bundled out by the constable. And the Overseers were as nervous as kittens if a single woman appeared on the scene, for fear she should become pregnant. And this was understandable, for a bastard became settled in the parish where (to use their phrase) he was 'dropped', and not like a normal child in the parish of his father. In a case like this, the alternatives were either the pass-cart or the shot-gun wedding. Parson Woodforde received 10s. 6d. for performing one of these in 1769. 'I married Tom Bunge of Amsford to Charity Andrews of Castle Cary by License this morning', he writes. 'The Parish of Cary made him marry her, and he came handcuffed to Church for fear of running away'. Since Tom lived in another parish, the Overseers had successfully passed the baby.

WORKING AND LIVING CONDITIONS

The lucky ones with jobs worked long hours. In large firms like Ambrose Crowley's, the men put in a 12- or 13-hour day. Domestic workers, able to please themselves, tended to alternate between bouts of 16 or 17 hours a day and spells of idle dissipation. In the long summer days, nail-makers or weavers could slave from six in the morning till 11 at night. After a day or two of this they would be attacked by what Francis Place remembered as that 'sickening aversion which at times steals over the working-man and utterly disables him. . . . I have felt it, resisted it to the utmost of my power, but have been obliged to submit and run away from my work. This is the case with every workman I have ever known'. Long hours were considered vital by the mercantilists in order to secure a favour-

Coalming, c. 1795

able balance of trade. For the same reason, the pundits favoured low wages and high food prices. 'Everyone but an idiot knows', wrote Arthur Young, 'that the lower classes must be kept poor or they will never be industrious.'

It is not easy to make out what Georgian wages were. They varied from place to place. They were higher in the town than in the country; higher in the south than in the north, and highest in London. They also fluctuated from time to time. An agricultural labourer might make 5s. a week in winter, 8s. in summer, and perhaps 12s. during the harvest. Since piece-rates were so common, much depended on the yards of cloth woven or pairs of stockings knitted. Skilled men received about half as much again as labourers. Miners on the Newcastle coalfield and engine-men in Shropshire ironworks would get 15s. a week, while their labourers would make 8s. or 9s. On the other hand, the labourer's wife and children might bring his total income to nearly twice that amount. In any case, everyone had perquisites, which make the raw wage-figures only a rough guide to total earnings. The farm-labourer often received his board and lodging, the miner his load of coal and the iron-worker his ale. Servants probably doubled their wages with tips, quite apart from their right to their master's cast-off clothes, and the Christmas gifts they drew from all his tradesmen: so much in the pound on all he had spent. The groom of the chambers at Canons, the home of the Duke of Chandos, used to make £38 a year solely out of showing visitors round. Thus no one can pronounce with any confidence on Georgian wages. And the same applies to real wages, for similar uncertainties bedevil the task of constructing a cost-of-living index. The most one can say is that, when the humanitarians began to grieve over the workers' conditions at the end of the century, they were better than they had been at the start.

Whether housing improved is more doubtful, for there was an increasing pressure of population on space and building materials. The rural labourer lived in a two-roomed cottage, with a chamber above in the roof. In Wigston in Leicestershire, the houses were built on footings of small round stones, with mud walls and thatched roofs, using the minimum of wood.

Everything depended on what materials were locally available, and perhaps on a landlord's soft heart. After viewing the hovels at Warminster, near Stratford-upon-Avon ('mud without and wretchedness within'), the Hon. John Byng swore this to his diary: 'Upon *my estate*, there shall be no mud cottages.' Where stone or bricks were available dwellings were decent, as at Gilbert White's Selborne; but some wretches lived in holes in the ground, and William Savery, the visitor from

Early morning at Covent Garden

Philadelphia, saw the poor at Bridgnorth in Shropshire living in caves cut from the soft rock in the side of a hill.

In the towns conditions were no better. The respectable artisan and his family occupied one room usually; while less wealthy workers lived and worked in cellars and garrets. Various factors conspired to convert labourers' suburbs into rabbit warrens. Nottingham had to expand in upon itself because the town fields were unenclosed till 1845. The workers there were crammed into a rookery called the Back Side, where only one passage, Sheep Lane, was wide enough for a farm-cart. In

112

London, where the jam was worst, it was partly due to government bans on building, dating from Tudor and Stuart times. In these circumstances, illegal tenements were run up out of sight, in courts and alleys behind existing structures. Only jerry-building with flimsy materials was worth while to speculative builders under the constant threat of demolition by the authorities for breach of some by-law, or for a faulty title to the land, if not actual trespass. This explains why Johnson called London a place where 'falling houses thunder on your head'; and accounts for the mysterious ease with which political mobs pulled houses down at the slightest provocation.

Where there was no room to expand, houses were divided and subdivided. Everyone let rooms. A respectable single man like Benjamin Franklin could get one for 1s. 6d. a week. A normal family would only achieve a garret for that. And those who had rooms took in lodgers: 15 or 20 to a room in St Giles and Bloomsbury at 2d. a night. Some lodgers sub-let a portion of their bed on a weekly lease. The lowest of the low occupied the cellars, the cobbler sleeping by his last, and the green-meat woman's family bedding down among her vegetable-matter. Cellars were damp, if not wet, for London's sewers were not all they should have been. The inhabitants of one house in Spital Square used to punt themselves across from the cellar-steps in a wash-tub to draw their daily beer.

The stench from these bilges rose from the cellar-flaps to mingle with the thousand and one other odours that polluted the metropolitan air. Windows were taxed, and so the reek of bodies, unwashed blankets and rotting curtains did not escape till a sash was thrown up to allow a chamber-pot to be emptied, or till a milk-seller emerged to dump her night-soil on the heap of carrion on the corner. The Fleet Ditch, before it was covered over in the 'thirties, was the receptacle of dead

Communal grave

dogs and whatever offal the tripe-dressers, sausage-makers and catgut-spinners could not employ in their trades. All the creeks into which the Thames tide washed contributed their sickening smells. 'These filthy places', said a writer in 1722, who was interested in anti-plague precautions, 'receive all the sinks, necessary houses and drains from dye houses, wash houses, fell mongers, slaughter houses and all kinds of offensive trades; they are continually full of carrion and the most odious of all offensive stench proceeds from them.' It proceeded also from those churchyards where paupers were buried in large communal graves, which were left open as long as there was room for one more. 'How noisome the stench is that arises from these holes so stow'd with dead bodies', said a health expert in 1721, 'especially in sultry seasons and after rain, one may appeal to all who approach them.' Above, the air was dark with the fumes from the industries of this coal-burning city, surrounded as it was with a smoke-screen of brick-kilns in full blast.

In spite of the efforts of some city-fathers and benevolent landlords, living conditions improved little for the urban worker. On the other hand, the evidence suggests that his diet gained in variety, though regional variations before the canals and turnpikes were constructed must limit generalisation. Bread, cheese and beer seem to have been the basis. Generally, bread was baked from wheat and barley, or wheat and rye; though in the north-east they ate a rye or barley loaf, and in the north-west they were limited to oatmeal. Gradually during the century, more and more workers advanced to pure wheaten bread, so that at the end, innocent of dieticians' charts, they looked down on anything else. 'Rye and barley bread', said Arthur Young in 1767, 'are looked on with horror even by poor cottagers.'

Brewing

Meat was taken perhaps once a week; but over much of the country the food

114

was cold, and so not much in the way of vegetables was consumed, except in areas well supplied with timber or coal. Tea began the period as an upper-class luxury and ended it as a working man's necessity, much to the horror of the reforming societies. Already in the 'thirties, Dr Deering was complaining that at Nottingham 'almost every Seamer, Sizer and Winder will have her Tea in a morning . . . and even a common Washerwoman thinks she has not had a proper Breakfast without Tea and hot buttered White Bread'. The annual consumption of sugar

Beer-drinking

also rose, from four pounds a head at the start of the century, to eight pounds in the middle and 13 pounds at the end.

And the production of beer steadily outpaced the increase in population, and state control maintained a stable price. In London, porter was 3d. a quart till 1761 and 3$\frac{1}{2}d$. thereafter till 1799, when it moved up to 4d. Except for the gin-orgy of the 'twenties, 'thirties and 'forties, beer was the standard daily drink; and a wise one in view of the doubtful sources of drinking water. The citizens of Nottingham used a fluid which was pumped up by a joint-stock company from the River Leen, the main sewer of the town. It was providential that they possessed one alehouse to every 80 or so inhabitants. And they needed them, for the lower classes, like their betters, performed many of their daily tasks under alcoholic auspices. Benjamin Franklin recorded how his printing shop near Lincoln's Inn Fields always had a pot-boy in attendance. 'My companion at press', he says, 'drank every day a pint before breakfast, a pint at breakfast . . . a pint between breakfast and dinner, a pint in the afternoon about 6 o'clock, and another pint when he

115

Cock-fighting

had done his day's work.' The field-reeves of Wigston chalked themselves up a drink every time they hired a crow-scarer or took out the town plough; and the mug-rings are still visible on their account-books to confirm it. On a Saturday night, a working man received his wages in a public house; if he went on a journey he caught the wagon there; if he was out of work it was his employment-exchange. Even if he was sent to gaol, he could buy as much beer as he could afford on the premises. Smaller prisons were *in* public houses, like the old White Lyon in Southwark.

All diversions were likewise drink-centred. 'All the amusements of the working people of the metropolis were immediately connected with drinking', said Francis Place, '—chair-clubs, chanting-clubs, lottery-clubs, and every variety of club, intended for amusement were always held at public-houses.' In Chichester, according to a resident, farmers coming in to market used 'to get drunk and stay two or three days till their wives came to fetch them Home'. In rural Northumberland there was a pre-Christian atmosphere about the way Whit Monday's racing was rounded off. 'They ended their recreation with Carrouzing at the Ale-houses', says a diarist, 'and ye men Kissing and toying away most of the night with their Mistresses. Some with their real Sweethearts and others with their Ladys of Pleasure.' Many ale-houses kept a pond for duck-hunting, and customers in the Tottenham Court Road area used to divert themselves by throwing a cat in and setting their dogs on it.

Any fight to the death between members of the brute creation drew a large crowd, and cock-fighting and bull-baiting were in great demand. In the churchyards of Chichester on Shrove

116

Tuesday throwing stones at a cock tied to a stake at three shots for 2*d.* was a great draw; and the rector of Bethnal Green in the East End of London used to complain about his parishioners' devotion to 'bullock-hanking' during divine service. 'I have seen them', he said, 'drive the animal through the most populous parts of the parish, force sticks pointed with iron up the body, put peas into the ears, and infuriate the beast, so as to endanger the lives of all persons passing along the streets.' But human suffering was even more popular. Parson Woodforde gave his servants time off to see a hanging in Norwich; London journeymen *took* a day off every six weeks to enjoy the Tyburn executions.

CRIME

Punishment may have suited the mood of brutalised cockneys, but it scarcely fitted the crime. There were few murders, but many executions; for most offences were against property. Burglary, arson and highway robbery hit Georgian society where it hurt most, and it let fly in a blind panic. New capital offences were created in a wild stampede: 33 under George II and 63 in the first 50 years of George III. With little or no debate, Parliament raised the number of capital crimes from about 50 at the start of the period to about 200 at the end. You could be hanged for picking a pocket to the value of 12 pence, or for being found in the company of gipsies. Setting fire to a town or to a heap of hay brought the same Nemesis. This was one half of the upper-class response to the swelling army of criminals; the other was the self-help of the property-owner. 'One is forced to travel, even at noon', Horace Walpole told Horace Mann, 'as if one was going to battle.' The real solution—an efficient

Jonathan Wild being carted through the streets, 1725

police-force—was not available to Lockeians with their healthy fear of adding to the powers of the state.

The severity of the criminal law impressed visitors from Continental tyrannies, but public executions horrified them. Even before the saturnalia at Tyburn, Londoners used to slip the keepers at Newgate a few coins just to stare at the condemned man. About 3,000 saw M'Lean the highwayman—and not only the plebs. 'I am almost single in not having been to see him', said Horace Walpole. 'Lord Mountford, at the head of half White's, went the first day.' Then came the two-hour journey by cart to the gallows, the manacled prisoner dressed in his best and sitting on his own coffin. In view of all the toasts he drank with the yelling crowds lining the route, he was mercifully pretty drunk for the horrible proceedings at Tyburn, where thousands more had bought seats in a grandstand erected by Widow Proctor, the cow-keeper who owned the site. And he would know nothing about the sale of his hangman's rope at 6d. an inch; nor would he feel the eyes of the oglers who thronged to see him dissected at Surgeons' Hall.

This exploitation of the baser instincts of the London populace was viewed quite calmly by the authorities. Indeed, the publicity was the whole point. 'Sir', said Dr Johnson, a humane man, 'executions are intended to draw spectators. If they do not draw spectators they don't answer their purpose.' The pillory, the whipping at the cart's tail, the suspending of the criminal's body in chains from a gibbet—all were supposed to be deterrent. The idea that he would be 'anatomised' was believed to be especially frightening to a would-be thief. However, the mounting total of hangings, reaching a record of 97 in 1785 in London and Middlesex alone, indicates flaws in this diagnosis.

The real cause of the increase of robberies, apart from the lack of police, was thought by foreigners to be the co-existence of wealth and poverty on one another's door-steps. 'It appears to me wonderful', wrote the German visitor Johann Archenholtz, 'that the crowds of poor wretches who continually fill the streets of the metropolis, excited by the luxurious and effeminate life of the great, have not some time or another entered

118

into a general conspiracy to plunder them.' But his fears were not realised in Georgian times, for the lower classes, for the most part, still made their protest in the form of rugged individualism. They did engage in politics at times, of course, but their aggressive emotions were usually exploited by members of the ruling circles for their own ends, like Bolingbroke and Wilkes. That is, until the violence culminating in the Gordon Riots of 1780 made the upper classes realise what fire they had been playing with. After that, the lower classes set up in politics on their own account; but even then most rioters aimed, not at the general overthrow of the established order, but at the righting of some particular wrong.

'Suppose the rich grind the face of the poor', asked John Wesley, 'what remedy against such oppression can he find in a Christian country?' The remedy was usually the sudden outburst of sticks and stones, and broken heads, and houses in flames. In 1749 the mob uprooted turnpikes in Bristol; in 1758 they tore down enclosures in Wiltshire. In Norwich in 1740 there was a five-day riot over the price of mackerel; at Leicester in 1766 the crowd stopped every wagon entering the town and

The Gordon Riots: burning of Aldgate Prison

Learning to read

sold the goods at their own prices. At Kettering in 1740 a 500-a-side football match evolved into an attack on a near-by mill. Matthew Boulton was attacked by 400 starving Cornish copper-miners in 1787. He only saved his life by giving them 20 guineas for drink. His partner James Watt thought this soft and said he should have called out the troops. Methodist-baiting often made the rabble go berserk: John Wesley records at least 60 riots in his Journals.

EDUCATION

Insolent and aggressive though they could be, the lower classes accepted the existing structure of society and government till the last decades of the century. One reason why they did not play at politics was their lack of education. Much was done by private charity to remedy this, but only a small impression was made on the prevailing ignorance. The upper and middle classes were faced with the perennial problem: how to teach the masses to be useful workers and upright citizens, without enabling them to compete with their own children, and without poisoning them with political aspirations. The Charity School movement (an outlet for middle-class zeal mentioned in the last chapter) was always on the horns of this dilemma. Under the auspices of the S.P.C.K., groups of subscribers founded a large number of these schools, especially in the first half of the period. The object was to spread virtue among the poor by teaching them to read. It was hoped that they would then soak themselves in the Bible, the Catechism and the *Whole Duty of Man*. That the urchins should grow up to read the *Rights of Man* was not part of the programme. On the contrary, they were to be taught, to quote Isaac Watts, 'to know what their station in life is, how mean

120

their circumstances, how necessary 'tis for them to be diligent, laborious, honest and faithful, humble and submissive, what duties they owe to the rest of mankind and particularly to their superiors'. Also on the curriculum was a little writing and arithmetic and a good deal of spinning, knitting and other lowly tasks. An enthusiastic London vicar thought that the Charity School alumni were 'as much distinguished from what they were before as is a tamed from a wild beast'; but cynical Bernard Mandeville doubted whether learning led to virtue. 'Vice in general', he wrote, 'is nowhere more predominant than where arts and science flourish.' If we may believe the accounts of the Methodists and Evangelicals, paganism was gaining on the Charity Schools by mid-century.

But literacy was growing. Although only a small fraction of the poor—perhaps 40,000 a year—went through their hands, the Charity Schools were an important supplement to the existing educational resources: the older endowed schools, the moribund apprenticeship system, the dame schools and the village curates. A snowball of literacy was started which was to roll on to menacing size. As we shall see, the religious reformers and the Sunday schools added their layers. And the Industrial Revolution sharpened the wits and transformed the habits of a skilled élite who knew what 1789 was all about when it came. By that time the lower classes were on the move. They were no longer content to leave their political and social welfare in the hands of their betters.

Further Reading

G. D. H. Cole and Raymond Postgate, *The Common People, 1746–1946*, University Paperbacks, 1961.
M. D. George, *England in Transition*, Pelican, 1953.
— — *London Life in the Eighteenth Century*, 1925, or London School of Economics reprints, 1951.
J. J. Hecht, *The Domestic Servant Class in Eighteenth-Century England*, 1956.
W. G. Hoskins, *The Midland Peasant*, 1957.
R. F. Wearmouth, *Methodism and the Common People of the Eighteenth Century*, 1945.

V

Cultural Life

SCIENCE

'There is no occupation more worthy and delightful', wrote John Ray the biologist, 'than to contemplate the beauteous works of nature and honour the infinite wisdom and goodness of God.' And this accurately conveys the atmosphere of Georgian intellectual life. During the generation before George I arrived in England, a profound mental convulsion occurred, the results of which are still unfolding. The scientific revolution wrenched the Western mind out of its old rut, placed it on new rails and sent it careering into the modern world. The genius of Newton absorbed post-Renaissance experimental data, mathematical skill and abstract speculation, and reduced it to a few laws of beautiful simplicity and immense range. They seemed to provide an exact explanation of the behaviour of every speck of matter in the universe: the stars in the sky and the particles on the earth.

> *Nature and Nature's Laws lay hid in Night:*
> *God said, Let Newton be! and all was Light.*

And Pope's life spans the vital years when the new outlook spread to the educated classes. It is a watershed in intellectual history; and Georgian culture is a joy-ride over the new territory. Poets and painters, parsons and political thinkers, doctors and mechanics, all went confidently forward in Newton's light, and in the glow provided by the bonfire of medieval superstition and dogma.

In physics, the picture sketched by Newton suffered little

change during our period, and
scientific advance was a matter
of filling in details provided by
more accurate observations and
more sophisticated mathematical
skills, though the latter were
mainly a Continental development. The growing-point of
physics was electricity. In 1709,
Francis Hauksbee developed the
first efficient friction-machine
for producing static electricity.

Sir Isaac Newton

This was the start of a century of European-wide experiments and
parlour-tricks with electric sparks. Stephen Gray established
the difference between conductors and insulators, and in 1730
electrified a boy suspended from the ceiling by threads made of
hair. In 1752, Benjamin Franklin proved by his famous kite
experiment that lightning was a gigantic electric spark—beating
the Russians by a year. His theoretical work produced a satisfactory explanation of the distinction between positive and
negative electricity; and his practical flair the lightning-con-
ductor.

Another basic advance was Priestley's inspiration that
electricity works according to the same law as gravitation:
that is, that the attraction or repulsion between two electric
charges is inversely proportional to the square of the distance
between them. While, in the meantime, the aristocratic recluse,
Henry Cavendish, was pioneering ways of measuring electric
currents and formulating concepts like what is now called
'potential'. But he did not publish all his results, and many
had to be rediscovered in the next century by men like Faraday.
Towards the end of our period, attention was switched from
static to current electricity—a move made possible by the
Italian Volta's invention of a simple electric cell. In England,
Sir Humphry Davy made important discoveries in the border
territory between electricity and chemistry. By means of
electrolysis, he decomposed caustic potash and caustic soda
and found two new metals, potassium and sodium.

Astronomical demonstration with an orrery

This was typical of the history of chemistry in the Georgian period, when many new substances were isolated for the first time. This was the century when chemistry was revolutionised, as physics had been under the Stuarts; and progress was due partly to improved experimental techniques (especially the use of quantitative methods) and partly to some inspired theorising in France by Lavoisier, the Newton of this story. The British contribution was mainly practical, and valuable information was collected by a variety of experimenters who regarded their work as a gentlemanly hobby. Stephen Hales, the perpetual curate of Teddington, among other things invented an apparatus for collecting gases over water. The Scots professor, Joseph Black, followed up this crucial advance by the rigorous use of the balance at every stage of his experiments. This enabled him to discover a new gas, now called carbon dioxide. He discovered that a given weight of chalk released the same quantity of this gas, whether by heating or by the addition of a dilute acid. He also discovered that there was a small quantity of it in the atmosphere. This represented an entirely new appreciation of the role of gases in the composition of matter, and triggered off a long period of investigation into the nature of 'air', which could no longer be regarded as a simple substance.

Advance in this field was first of all assisted, and then blocked, by a concept which eventually had to be jettisoned. This was phlogiston, an inflammable principle, which the German professor Stahl postulated was released into the air whenever anything burned. The ash was the original substance minus its phlogiston. When quantitative methods showed the residue to be heavier than the original substance (owing, as we should say, to the absorption of oxygen on burning) Georgian chemists saved the theory by giving phlogiston a negative weight. Much fruitful experimentation was stimulated by the mental gymnastics involved in accommodating this mythical substance, with the results coming out mirror-fashion compared with the modern view. Where we say 'oxygen', they said 'minus phlogiston', and so on. Priestley actually collected some oxygen, and realised that it supported life and combustion better than air. But he could not take the plunge and called it 'dephlogisticated air'. When Lord Shelburne (his patron at that time) took him to Paris in 1774, he mentioned his find to Lavoisier at dinner one day. The latter's mind was less muscle-bound, and after a bout of intense experimentation he succeeded in making the theoretical somersault. Phlogiston was thrown overboard. The one-fifth of the atmosphere which burning things absorbed he called 'oxygen'; and the remaining four-fifths he named 'azote'—in English, 'nitrogen'.

In biology, no fundamental reappraisal occurred till the nineteenth century, for the Georgian period was only the great fact-collecting stage. Darwin's insights would have been impossible without the material accumulated by observers like his grandfather, Erasmus Darwin, or Gilbert White of Selborne, or Joseph Banks, who went with Cook to Australia and gave Botany Bay its name. In the early years of the period, the Rev. Stephen Hales published his findings in plant-physiology in his *Vegetable Staticks*. Towards the end, John Hunter, the famous surgeon, placed comparative anatomy on firm foundations with his dissections of hundreds of different species of animals and plants. But England's contribution was modest compared with, say, Buffon's *Histoire Naturelle*; and undoubtedly the greatest single step forward was made by the Swedish botanist, Carl Linnaeus. He classified plants according to their stamens and pistils, and divided them into *genera* and *species*, the basis of his double-naming system which he got universally accepted. He believed that each species was descended from an original created by God (as men were descended from Adam); and, though he had second thoughts in later life, he under-pinned the belief in the immutability of the species—the chief mental barrier to the acceptance of Darwin's thesis. Nevertheless, his

Chemist

system of identification made for rapid progress over the whole field of biological studies.

In no branch of science was the amateur more confidently expert than in medicine; and we find that every diary- and letter-writer had his own witches' broth and patent cure-alls. William Byrd from Virginia recommended rattlesnake root for 'the pleurisy, the rheumatism, and easing of pain in any part that proceeds from inflammation'. 'I drank snail tea for breakfast', wrote the Hon. John Byng, 'for my chest is very sore.' Henry Fox believed in taking medicines 'in postures that should make them long in travelling through one's body, instead of hurrying them through, post'. Lord Buckinghamshire dipped his gouty foot in cold water and killed himself. Georgian medicine lacked its Linnaeus, and the confused nomenclature tended to make treatment a hit-and-miss affair. There was a rich variety of fevers: spotted, putrid, brain, low, relapsing, intermittent and continued—to mention only a few. A small boy with a rash wrote home from his school near High Wycombe to say that the school doctor 'calls it the blisters, not the chicken pox and says that the chicken pox, the watry jags, the Blisters and swine Pox are all the same Disorder under different names'.

At the professional level there was much progress to record. The plague had disappeared for good; inoculation checked smallpox and vaccination conquered it. The link between dirt and disease was grasped, and better hygiene reduced gaol-fever and made child-birth less of a gamble with death. Midwifery progressed as the lying-in hospitals were founded; and a large number of general hospitals were started by philanthropists all over the country. In these, fundamental knowledge was discovered and passed on to successive generations of better educated practitioners, though the best medical schools were still outside England. Hospitals were free, though, in the

Georgian way, you usually had to know someone who knew a governor before you could get in. At St Bartholomew's, you also had to put down 19s. 6d. for burial fees. This was returnable, of course, if you recovered. Surgical skill also became more widespread, particularly when William Hunter began to add demonstrations and dissections to his lectures. Operations were conducted without drugs, except brandy; but they were not so hideously painful as they might seem. William Cheselden at St Thomas's often extracted a stone from the bladder in less than half a minute.

Newton survived into Georgian England, but the period produced no other scientific genius. In fact, the country owes its triumphs not to the concentration of talent in one or two great men, but to the wide dispersal of the scientific habit of mind among the people. When the truth is known, perhaps this characteristic more than any other will account for the precocity of England's economic growth. For the Industrial Revolution was a whole collection of scientific experiments. The brewers and distillers, bleachers and dyers, pot-throwers and iron-smelters must be accorded a place in Georgian science; and so must the men who built the roads and machines, or boosted the yield of meat and grain. Nor were these technological advances the product of unlettered trial and error, as is sometimes imagined. There were ample arrangements for business-men, scientists and technicians to pick one another's brains; and the cross-fertilization of ideas between John Roebuck, Joseph Black and James Watt on the steam-engine was not exceptional. Wedgwood supplied utensils for Priestley's chemical experiments, while Priestley investigated minerals of possible use at Etruria.

Manufacturers who joined the Manchester Literary and

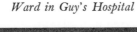

Ward in Guy's Hospital

Philosophical Society could tap the knowledge of six Fellows of the Royal Society among their colleagues. One member, John Dalton, taught at the Manchester Academy using Lavoisier's *Elements of Chemistry* as a text-book. The importance of the academies has already been stressed; but the adult thirst for self-improvement was just as significant. Practically every town had its regular visits from itinerant lecturers, like Dr Thomas Garnett, whose lectures on chemistry, according to the *Manchester Mercury*, were on its 'Application to the common purposes of life, as well as to the useful Arts of Bleaching, Dyeing, Agriculture, etc.'.

PHILOSOPHY

The scientific outlook was not limited to merchandise, but penetrated every nook and cranny of Georgian intellectual life. 'It would be very singular', wrote Voltaire, who spread its influence on the Continent, 'that all nature, all the planets, should obey eternal laws, and that there should be a little animal, five feet high, who, in contempt of these laws, could act as he pleased, solely according to his caprice.' The philosophers were all confident that what Newton had done for physics, they could do for psychology, morals, sociology, politics, aesthetics and religion. Collect enough facts, they thought, discover the laws that God has built into the human condition, and the perfectibility of man would be in sight. This was the essence of the Age of Reason, and it was characterised in England by empiricism rather than rationalism. A Georgian philosopher did not balance a metaphysical mountain on an axiom or two; but, following Locke, derived a few probable truths from a vast array of facts.

Locke's unemotional approach, tolerant attitude, common-sense language and factual bias set the tone for the whole century. His rejection of 'innate ideas'; his sensationalist psychology; his reduction of human motives to the pursuit of pleasure and the avoidance of pain; his hope of placing 'morality among the sciences capable of demonstration'; his social-contract theory of politics; his belief in the 'reasonableness of Christianity'; his support of Toleration: all formed the points from

128

which later thinkers started. But they produced such an abundance of bold formulations and seminal insights that a mere sketch will have to suffice here.

Now that the old Christian certainties had been undermined, the Georgians were intensely interested in finding a new basis for morals; and life for most of them was not a matter of resisting the Devil, or suffering the burden of Original Sin, or fleeing from the wrath to come, but finding happiness. 'To say truth', wrote Soame Jenyns, 'Happiness is the only thing of real value in existence: neither riches, nor power, nor wisdom, nor learning, nor strength, nor beauty, nor virtue, nor religion, nor even life itself, being of any importance but as they contribute to its production.' Of course, the pursuit of happiness was not the same as chasing every passing pleasure; for the good man could distinguish between his short-term and his long-term felicity. But how did they deal with the evident possibility of a clash between one man's happiness and another's, or that of society as a whole? Some postulated a kind of Newtonian law which harmonised the true long-term happiness of each with that of all.

The chief source of this optimistic view of the universe was Lord Shaftesbury's influential *Characteristicks of Men, Manners, Opinions, Times*, the chief ingredients of which formed the basis of Pope's *Essay on Man:*

> *Thus God and Nature link'd the gen'ral frame,*
> *And bade Self-love and Social be the same.*

Evil, according to this view, is an illusion caused by our inability to see the whole picture:

> *All Discord, Harmony not understood:*
> *All partial Evil, universal Good;*
> *And, spite of Pride, in erring Reason's spite,*
> *One truth is clear*, Whatever is, *is* right.

Thus human poverty and pain are massaged away by Soame Jenyns (whose book was thrashed by Johnson in a review) with the theory 'that the sufferings of individuals are absolutely necessary to universal happiness'. The fact that in everyday life virtue and happiness often fail to coincide was a great inconvenience to these thinkers. It was offset by theologians like Paley with rewards and punishments after death. Another way round the difficulty was to postulate, with Hutcheson, a benevolence in man which can recognise and seek 'the greatest happiness of the greatest number'.

This characteristic devotion to things as they stood also rings through all the hymns to the British constitution, founded on the Revolution Settlement and the Protestant Succession. With the old prop of Divine Right knocked away, Georgian political theorists concentrated at first on finding an alternative justification for political authority, based on reason instead of faith. Locke's solution, again, was found generally acceptable, with its contract theory, its defence of property, its belief in government by consent, in toleration, in the minimal state, the separation of powers and the ultimate right of resistance to tyranny. With the foundations agreed on, theorists then began to consider the other end of the problem: what governments ought to do.

The answers were such as one would expect in the intellectual climate of the time. The Scot, Adam Smith, in his *Wealth of Nations*, founded the science of political economy on a philosophy which harmonised well with the *Essay on Man*. If each man pursued his own self-interest, he believed, there was a principle inherent in economic life (the 'invisible hand') which ensured that this produced the greatest good for all. It followed, then, that for governments it was 'the highest impertinence to pretend to watch over the economy of private people'. Similarly, Jeremy Bentham judged political action by its results, and his criterion is the hedonistic principle we have already noticed. 'It is the greatest happiness of the greatest number', he said, 'that is the measure of right and wrong.' All institutions which failed to achieve this were to be thrown out and new ones created that did. Not much in the way of government action to implement this view can be credited to the Hanoverian period, but the influence of these Georgian theorists on Victorian practice was immense.

It was a blessing for eighteenth-century self-confidence, that two of the subtlest thinkers of the time, Berkeley and Hume,

130

were not widely read, for they posed
problems which have had philosophers
running round in circles ever since.
Berkeley, a delightful Irish bishop and
elegant stylist with a leaning towards
mysticism, pursued the empiricist tracks
into very difficult terrain—beyond the
point where Locke had stopped short.
If all that Locke knew were sense-data,
how could he know of the independence
of objects which produced them? Berkeley
argued that ideas were the only things
we could be sure of, and that the ex-
ternal world depended for its existence
on being perceived. But tables and chairs
did not go in and out of existence
according to whether we perceived them

George Berkeley, Bishop of Cloyne

or not: their continuance was guaranteed by the fact that they
were constantly perceived by the mind of God.

One has doubts about including Hume here, for he was a
Scot, who wrote his masterpiece, *The Treatise of Human
Nature*, in Paris, and was celebrated in the Georgian period
primarily as a historian. He drove right through rationalism
and came out the other side—a complete sceptic. He dug below
the foundations of that reason which the eighteenth century
thought would solve all problems, and found that they rested on
sand. He not only demolished miracles, but even made untenable
the argument from design, on which, as we shall see, the Deists
depended for the belief in the existence of a deity. Not content
with denying the possibility of reason discovering a deductive
morality, he dethroned reason altogether from its governing
role in moral action. 'Reason is, and ought only to be', he said,
'the slave of the passions, and can never pretend to any other
office than to serve and obey them.' And before he had finished
he had laid waste every inch of empiricist territory by with-
holding the certificate of certainty from every particle of our
inductive knowledge. The assumption of causation, upon which
the whole of science depended, was grounded, according to

him, on nothing firmer than coincidence. 'All our reasonings concerning causes and effects are deriv'd from nothing but custom', he said.

How did a philosophic mind survive such nuclear destruction? Hume fell back on common-sense. 'I dine, I play a game of backgammon, I converse, and am merry with my friends; and when, after three or four hours' amusement, I wou'd return to these speculations, they appear so cold, and strain'd, and ridiculous, that I cannot find in my heart to enter into them any farther.'

RELIGION

The intellectual atmosphere of the century following Newton and Locke did not encourage an intense religious life. Nor, on the other hand, did it lead to atheism. The argument from design convinced most, whether Deist, Latitudinarian or Dissenter. 'The works of Nature', said Locke, 'everywhere sufficiently evidence a Deity.' Deists like Tindal, Bolingbroke or Tom Paine believed in 'natural religion', deduced by reason from the facts of nature. Revelation was unnecessary; mysterious matters like the miracles or the prophecies were against common-sense. A benevolent deity had set the universe going and then left it to its own devices, they said. But deism was never very strong in England, partly because Christians like Butler and sceptics like Hume had demolished its arguments; and partly because (unlike in France) the Established Church was only a logical step or two away from it.

Baptism

The Latitudinarians believed that 'natural religion' was incomplete without Revelation, which was also reasonable. The title of Locke's treatise, *The Reasonableness of Christianity*, sums up their position. And the sermons of Archbishop Tillotson (the favourite reading of the Augustan Church) epitomise their cool, tolerant and prosaic attitude to religious life. His sermons on *His commandments are not grievous* and *The advantage of religion to societies* are two examples of the tendency to reduce Christianity to good behaviour in everyday life. The preoccupation of the Georgians with social morality is here again apparent. Horace Walpole went to church only to set an example to the servants. 'A good moral sermon may instruct and benefit them', he said.

Church service

'Enthusiasm' was disdained: it was irrational, it was vulgar and it smacked of the religious turmoil of the previous age, now happily over for a church secure in the Protestant Succession.

After the rebellion of 1715, Dudley Ryder heard the Bishop of Salisbury preach 'a very good honest sermon full of abhorrence of the rebellion and all popish principles'. Aspiring clergy had to toe the right political line, for the grandees, like Newcastle, who controlled the state machine, made promotion depend on it. William Warburton provided theoretical foundations in his *Alliance between Church and State*. 'The Church shall apply all its Influence in the service of the State', he wrote, '. . . the State shall support and protect the Church.' The consequence was pluralism and absenteeism, and fashionable parsons like Johnson's school-friend, Dr Taylor. 'His size, and figure, and countenance, and manner', says Boswell, 'were that of a hearty English 'Squire, with the parson super-induced.' Such clerics spent their stipends on society and politics, and hired a curate at £40 a year to do their ecclesiastical chores for them. And the situation steadily deteriorated with rapid industrialisation. With the growth and movement of the masses, the distribution of churches came to have about as much relation to population-density as the Parliamentary constituencies. It was thus not surprising that 'knees and hassocks are well-nigh divorc'd', as Cowper put it.

The Nonconformist congregations, still suffering from civil disabilities, but secure in their toleration, were not immune from the prevailing tepid atmosphere. One member, Dudley Ryder, thought the differences between Dissent and the Establishment were 'very small and trifling'. 'For my own part', he said, 'I could communicate with either of them.' But in all churches there were bishops, parsons and pastors who performed their duties with zeal, and who carried the seventeenth-century religious warmth through into the Georgian period. And the highly intellectualised approach to religion could not satisfy human nature for ever, any more than it could in literature or philosophy. In any case, there was growing at the bottom of the social scale a mass of workers whose life was a savage struggle. They did not know anything about the intricacies of predestination, or the Trinity, or the argument from design; and did not want to know, either. They were thirsting for a warmer draught: for faith, which, as Wesley said in 1738, is 'not barely a speculative, rational thing, a cold lifeless assent, a train of ideas in the head, but also a disposition of the heart'.

The Evangelical Revival, which was visible from the 'forties onwards, affected Dissent and Church of England alike. The greatest inspiration for it was William Law's *A Serious Call to a Devout and Holy Life.* This was no essay in rational calculation, but a moving appeal to the heart. Here and there, ministers like Newton at Olney, Grimshaw at Haworth, Fletcher at Madeley and Simeon at Cambridge responded, and devoted their lives to the conversion of their flocks back to vital religion.

The most effective, of course, was John Wesley, who made the vital innovation of becoming an itinerant preacher. Altogether, he travelled a quarter of a million miles, preaching sometimes two or three sermons a day, to a handful in a village, or a crowd of 20,000 in an industrial town. Where the local parson was hostile, as he often was, he spoke outside in the fields. And his theme was not Augustan prudential morality, but 'plain, old Bible Christianity'; and he preached it with a dramatic force that swept thousands into a new mode of life. Sometimes his converts wept, and screamed and fell down in convulsions. But wherever he passed, he organised a small group of the faithful to carry on the work. For he was a powerful and inventive administrator, and gradually constructed a vast pyramid of control, based on the little 'bands' at the bottom. Then came the 'circuits' and 'districts', with the annual Conference at the top—all under his command.

This was all too much for the Church of England to stomach, particularly when he allowed laymen to administer the sacraments, and ordained ministers to serve in the newly independent

The mobbing of John Wesley at Wednesbury

Samuel Johnson

United States. Wesley himself wished his community to remain fully a part of the Church, but after his death the inevitable secession occurred. And the Methodist Church, together with the other Evangelical congregations, swelled into the most powerful of all the forces which were about to transform Georgian cultural life altogether.

LITERATURE

Georgian creative writers are now better appreciated than they were in Victorian times, when they were esteemed principally as models of what to avoid. They derived their characteristics partly from the intellectual atmosphere just described. The all-purpose philosophy of reason rolls smoothly through Pope's *Essay on Man*, so lubricated and sprung that no jolts are felt from stones left unturned and no sound is heard but the beat of the metre. And many lesser examples of this cerebral, ruminative, witty and tightly constructed verse provided aspiring gentry and merchants with predigested morsels of the prevailing ideology, untouched by Humean hands. But the nature of this literature was also partly due to the social context, and the place of the writer in it.

The social, political and religious violence of Stuart times was now over, and the great families controlled a society that seemed as stable as the Newtonian universe itself. They patronised writers who aimed to keep it that way. The literary world had expanded from the Court to the Town, but it was still intimate enough for poets to speak directly to a homogeneous audience, whose education had sensitised them to the classical echoes in the satires and pastorals, and whose knowledge of the world enabled them to catch the wicked references to contemporary scandal. Moreover, writers lived close to the hub of social and political life. They fraternised with the magnates in coffee-houses and routs, and depended partly on their patronage, as Swift did on Harley. Some magnates, like Chesterfield, Bolingbroke or Horace Walpole, were authors on their own account. Subject-matter in these circumstances tended to be public rather than private, social rather than individual, urban rather than rural. The poet was a man doing a job of work in the world rather than a visionary exploring his own soul. His business, said Johnson, was 'to examine, not the individual, but the species; to remark general properties and large appearances'. Poetry did not yet provide a substitute for religion, but polished up into pleasing form 'what oft was thought but ne'er so well expressed', as Pope put it. Johnson praised Gray's *Elegy* because it abounded 'with images which find a mirror in every mind, and with sentiments to which every bosom returns an echo'.

Politics, business, agriculture and all the daily concerns of man in society were proper subjects for verse, rather than the solitary imaginings of the sufferer grappling with his *Angst*. The head, not the heart, held the easy flow of the language and the precise unfolding of the thought within the confines of the heroic couplet. Poetic diction like Cowper's 'feather'd tribes domestic' and 'public hives of puerile resort' helped to preserve propriety. And the use of irony, puns, epigrams, parallelisms and antitheses indicate fancy rather than imagination. This was the Age of Reason; but Swift's savage indignation at the failure of the human race to rise to its possibilities, Pope's filthy smearing of his enemies, Johnson's fear of death and Cowper's conviction that he was marked for eternal damnation—all indicate what emotions were damped down beneath the exquisite surface.

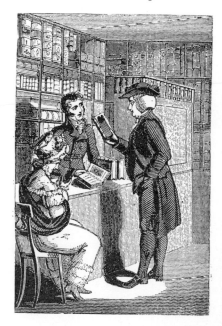

Bookseller's shop

And in the second half of the century, this surface began to crumble with the expansion of the business and professional classes. As the marketing of literature evolved from private patronage, through subscription publishing, to publishing

137

Oliver Goldsmith

by booksellers, the writer became less of a hired entertainer of the *haut monde* and more of an independent professional man. He was now alone, addressing an audience whose numbers were swelling, and whose wants were unpredictable. In these conditions, the conventions of Augustan literature could not go on for ever.

The new state of affairs is seen early in prose, and the sharp eye of Defoe was quick to notice. 'Writing', he said in 1725, '. . . is become a very considerable Branch of the English Commerce.' In this medium, the eighteenth century invented two new literary forms: the periodical-essay and the novel. Steele and Addison in their *Tatler* and *Spectator* started a fashion in Queen Anne's reign which Johnson and Goldsmith sustained under the Georges. Addison's aim was to bring 'philosophy out of closets and libraries, schools and colleges, to dwell in clubs and assemblies, at tea-tables and in coffee-houses'. And these essays steadily civilised the climbing gentlemen and merchants, improving their manners and morals, as well as clarifying their punctuation and pinning down their spelling. This stream of didacticism is one of the headwaters of middle-class morality, and Victorian tender-mindedness is clearly apparent in Addison.

It was a working journalist, outside the inner ring of patronised authors, who wrote the first full-scale narrative about real people against a real background. *Robinson Crusoe*, which came out in 1719, with three editions in four months, made over £1,000 for its publisher; and is now better known in every country in the world than Defoe is in his. In the 'forties, Richardson and Fielding raised fiction to a higher level with their fuller orchestration of character and plot, their comprehensive survey of the social scene and detailed analysis of the human psyche. Together with the picaresque Smollett full of vigorous incident, the off-centre Sterne with his cerebral sophistication,

138

and many other followers, they consolidated fiction into the most potent literary force of the modern world.

Little need be said of Georgian drama. Perhaps the middle-class invasion of the playhouse is the reason for the emasculated sentimentality of the tragedy and the deodorized gentility of the comedy. Perhaps good work could not be expected when the stage was partly occupied by the quality in their boxes; and

Drury Lane Theatre, designed by Robert Adam in 1773

when people dropped in for a scene or two mainly to gaze at the audience. William Byrd, the American, sometimes called in at a show or two on his way to the coffee-house. He found difficulty in keeping awake, unless there was an attractive girl in the audience. Perhaps dramatic illusion was hard to achieve when Covent Garden and Drury Lane had a row of spikes across the front of the stage; when Caesar was played in a full-bottom wig; when the spectators were free with their cat-calls and guffaws if they were not chatting with one another; and when

139

a shower of rotten fruit might be the prologue to an attempt to break the place up, benches, boxes, scenery and all. Perhaps it was the star-system, which Garrick exploited so well. Perhaps the blame can be laid on the pitiful remuneration which dramatists received: it left the field too free for wealthy amateurs like Gentlemen Johnny Burgoyne to get their works staged. Whatever the reason, apart from those of Colman, Goldsmith or Sheridan, Georgian plays are not often revived.

MUSIC

Upper-class audiences behaved little better at the opera. Here the composers, performers and conductors were mostly foreign. According to Hervey, musicians could make far more money in England than anywhere else in Europe. 'My countrymen', he said, 'give them £3,000 a year to come there to have the pleasure of hissing them off when they are there.' Music-lovers seemed less interested in the rule-ridden Italian operas than in forming cliques to support rival stars, like the two fighting prima donnas, Cuzzoni and Faustina. Open warfare finally broke out between the partisans of these two when hisses and cat-calls closed down Buononincini's *Astyanax* in June 1727. A later battle washed the steps of the throne—or rather the royal family were knee-deep in it. George II supported Handel at Covent Garden, while Frederick Prince of Wales and the opposition leaders formed a rival establishment at Lincoln's Inn Fields. When Handel, an inept political tactician, wrote an anthem for Frederick's marriage, the king dropped him like a hot brick, with the result that he and Covent Garden went bankrupt.

Harpsichordist

This was not Handel's only financial collapse, for he was used to a fickle public as well as a

George Frederick Handel

peevish monarch. His first three oratorios, *Esther*, *Deborah* and *Athaliah*, were hits; but then *Saul* and *Israel* fell flat; and London's reception of the *Messiah* was really hostile. The clergy, even, pronounced it irreligious. This was the pot calling the kettle black; but George II differed. He rose to his feet at the Hallelujah Chorus, inaugurating an English custom which still survives. Shortly after this, in the 'forties, Handel really moved back into favour, with his *Te Deum* to celebrate Dettingen, his *Judas Maccabaeus* to honour the defeat of the Forty-five, and his Music for the Royal Fireworks to salute the Peace of Aix-la-Chapelle.

In the second half of the period, the public began to support native talent. The early success of the *Beggar's Opera* (which was based on folk-tunes) had not been followed up; but in the 'sixties Thomas Arne, the only Georgian composer of any great merit, started the long vogue of the ballad opera with his *Love in a Village*. He directed the orchestra at Vauxhall Gardens; and the popularity of the concerts there and at Ranelagh (where Burney played the organ) and at Carlisle House in Soho (where J. C. Bach was in charge) supports the other evidence that all ranks found a deep pleasure in music, even if their taste was unsophisticated. Dr Johnson, who confessed that 'he was very insensible to the power of musick', was not typical. What does, perhaps, typify the modest Georgian talent in this field is the wealth of popular songs like 'Where the bee sucks' and 'Lass of Richmond Hill' which date from this period. The hymns tell the same story.

PAINTING

In the visual arts, Georgian deference to foreign standards was equally slavish. The Grand Tour was habit-forming, and the

London Magazine in 1733 complained that the dealers were 'continually importing shiploads of dead Christs, Holy Families, Madonnas, and other dismal dark subjects'. These found a welcome home in Palladian mansions. On the other hand, the England of the Protestant Succession and constitutional monarchy was temperamentally unfitted to reproduce the rhetoric of baroque Europe. The Georgian gentry were not prepared for 'poetical painting', according to Henry Fuseli, whose bent lay in that direction. 'Portrait with them is everything. Their taste and feelings all go to realities.' This quality is visible in the success of Kneller's standardised likenesses, Stubbs' exact delineation of horses and dogs, Joseph Wright of Derby's reproductions of scientific and industrial episodes, and the portraits and conversation-pieces of Hogarth, Reynolds, Gainsborough, Romney and the rest.

Reynolds lectured in support of the *gusto grande*; and painters (like writers) aimed at the 'general idea'. This justified them in 'elevating' their subjects, in modifying details of dress and appearance in order to bring out the 'nobler parts': say, the statesmanlike qualities of a cabinet-minister, or the seaworthiness of an admiral. Sometimes, this simply meant leaving out the warts. Queen Caroline told Zincke, the German enameller, not to make the king look more than 25. George told him not to make the queen look above 28—though she was about two years his junior. But Reynolds aimed at the ideal. In fact, 'face-painting' for him was inferior to the highest art of all—history-painting—at which the two Americans, West and Copley, were so successful. Fortunately, with Reynolds this was all theory; and his psychological intuition makes him as great as anyone painting in Europe at that time. Modern

William Hogarth

taste, perhaps, is more sympathetic to Gainsborough, with his more delicate touch, more sensitive insight into character, and his natural, rather than conventionalised, poses and backgrounds.

Certainly, Georgian taste did not appreciate the ruthless honesty of Hogarth's portraits; and fashionable people did not run the hazard of giving him

William Hogarth and David Garrick

commissions. On the other hand, the engravings of what Garrick called his 'pictur'd Morals' had a wide sale with the public at large. These sets of documentary social criticism were strikingly original. They were 'a field', Hogarth said, 'not broken up in any country or any age'—and well cultivated by Rowlandson and Gillray, and by cartoonists ever since. Like the full-blooded novels of his contemporary Fielding, they are Georgian England to the life.

ARCHITECTURE

The formation of the Royal Academy in 1768 heralded, not the hardening of Georgian art into its mould, but the break-up of standards which was bound to occur with the elevation of the artist to a professional level. It happened in literature; and a similar evolution can be seen in architecture. At the start of the period, architects tended to be under the thumb of the great magnates who patronised them. The Duchess of Marlborough, who found Vanbrugh too independent-minded at Blenheim, said that 'anybody that has sense, with the best workmen of all sorts, could make a better house without an architect'. Lord Burlington, and others, did. And he, more than anyone, set the fashion for patrician building for which Georgian England is renowned, and which its devotees can still enjoy, not only in London, Bristol or York, but also in Boston, Massachusetts, or Newport, Rhode Island.

Burlington returned from the Grand Tour in 1715 in love with the work of Palladio, the Italian Renaissance architect. His enthusiasm swung English building on to its new tack, helped by the influence of two books which began publication in the same year. These were *Vitruvius Britannicus,* by Colen Campbell, and the translation of Palladio's *I quattro libri dell' architettura,* with plates by Giacomo Leoni. The great Whig families preferred the clarity and balance of the new rules to the near-baroque of the previous age. Wren, Vanbrugh and Hawksmoor now seemed too theatrical and extravagant, smacking of popery and absolute monarchy. Official building naturally went the same way; and soon the Office of Works, which had been dominated till then by these three, was filled by Burlington men.

There followed an era of splendid architecture. Year after year, in every corner of the kingdom, country palaces and city mansions, churches and colleges, town-halls and customs-houses, farm-houses and assembly-rooms rose from the drawing-boards of Campbell, Leoni, Flitcroft, Kent (the genius of the group) and lesser men following their lead. Counterpoint was provided by Gibbs, who built more in the Wren tradition. One brilliant innovation was the treatment of whole rows of houses as single units in the classical manner. Grosvenor

North Parade, Bath, in 1777

Square in the 'thirties began a style of town-planning which was followed by other London streets and squares, and wonderfully exploited in the circuses and crescents of centres like Bath and Buxton and Brighton, which had the good fortune to expand rapidly in the latter part of this period.

Later Georgian times saw an advance in the status of the architect. He ceased to get his board and lodging as part of a noble retinue, and became an independent virtuoso, courted by the great. At the same time, Augustan certainties began to waver. Historical research was revealing that classical architecture was much less hide-bound than the version of it which the Renaissance had handed on. An appreciation of medieval work also emerged, and a taste for Chinese and Indian styles. The late-Georgian architect thus has a wider choice of styles to exploit, and, with the expansion of the business community, a more varied clientele to satisfy. The way was clear for the more eclectic work of Sir William Chambers, the personal manner of Robert Adam, and the architectural free-for-all with which the period ended.

Further Reading

H. Butterfield, *The Origins of Modern Science*, 1957.
A. R. Hall, *The Scientific Revolution*, 1954.
Basil Willey, *The Eighteenth Century Background*, 1940.
G. R. Cragg, *The Church and the Age of Reason*, Pelican, 1961.
N. Sykes, *Church and State in England in the Eighteenth Century*, 1934.
David Daiches, *A Critical History of English Literature*, Vol. II, 1961.
Boris Ford (ed.), *The Pelican Guide to English Literature*, Vol. 4: *From Dryden to Johnson*, 1957.
E. K. Waterhouse, *Painting in Britain, 1530–1790*, Pelican History of Art, 1953.
J. N. Summerson, *Architecture in Britain, 1530–1830*, Pelican History of Art, 1953.

VI

The End of
Georgian England

The beginning of the end of the Georgian era is plainly visible
in the early 'eighties. In those years, the graphs of economic
activity took a sharp turn upwards. In 1782, Watt took out a
patent for the Sun and Planet gear, which enabled his steam-
engine to turn machinery. In 1783 the American colonies gained
their independence, the younger Pitt became Prime Minister,
and Charles James Fox advanced the novel constitutional opinion
that the House of Commons could tell the king what ministers
to appoint. In 1784, Cartwright invented his power-loom;
Dr Johnson died; and Henry Cort took out his puddling and
rolling patent for the mass-production of wrought iron. In
1785, Pitt introduced a motion for parliamentary reform; the
first steam-driven spinning mill opened; and Wilberforce was
converted to Evangelicalism. The rate of social change accelerated; and in 1789 the fall of the Bastille began a series of
traumatic experiences, after which neither England nor Europe
could ever be the same again.

POLITICS

The personal authority of the monarch was on the wane. The
failure of the American war, to which George III was so
personally committed, threw him into the hands of his enemies,
the Rockingham Whigs, who were out to win back for the
great aristocratic families the power they had enjoyed under the
Pelhams during George II's old age. The programme of Economical Reform, which they forced down the king's throat, aimed

146

at reducing royal patronage and rousing 'Country' support, so that they could rule undisturbed. George out-manœuvred them, and eventually found what he thought was his man. Pitt formed a minority government in late 1783, and he and the king obstinately survived the attacks of Fox and Burke, while John Robinson organised the election of March, 1784. This, in time-honoured Georgian fashion, produced a House of Commons' majority for the new ministers. But this victory was as much the result of popular support as royal influence, for the body of

George III

voters were not yet willing to see the royal power pared down to Victorian size. Fox was too far ahead of them; and, in any case, they had been thoroughly scared by the radical movement.

This began in the 'sixties and 'seventies, when the libel-trials of Wilkes, the refusal of the House of Commons to let him sit for Middlesex, the dispute with the Americans and the Irish made it appear that the corrupt Georgian parliament was more dangerous to liberty than the Stuart kings had been. These struggles led to some bold re-thinking over the whole range of political institutions. They brought to the surface a liberal tradition which had been steadily flowing underground since the seventeenth century, and which was swollen now by rationalistic schemes from the Continental Enlightenment. For these theorists, 1688 had not gone far enough; but they were supported by many more who were only anxious to return the constitution to its Revolutionary purity.

For the radical movement at first seemed to be another of those respectable 'Country', 'Patriot' or 'Tory' crowds, which opposition politicians had long been used to bringing out on the streets to serve their own ends. But when it started

147

John Wilkes

to paddle its own canoe, to demand parliamentary reform, and to exploit new methods of agitation like mass-meetings, remonstrances and instructions to M.P.s, the machine-politicians and the country-gentry began to have second thoughts. And when it organised itself into an Association on a nation-wide scale, and when its big campaign of 1779 led to the Gordon Riots in 1780 (when London was at the mercy of a drunken mob for several days), the Rockinghams and the Shelburnes, and even the Wilkeses, realised they had bitten off more than they could chew.

The mass of the people rallied round Pitt and the throne. The French Revolution confirmed their loyalty, and the ensuing war stiffened it with patriotism. It was the radical philosopher, Joseph Priestley, whose house was burned down by the mob in the Birmingham riots. But the radical movement was not dead. The year 1780 left behind a hard core of agitators—idealists and cranks, liberal-minded aristocrats and angry working-men, radical Dissenters and atheistic planners—who built upon the imperishable experience of that year. They were given new hope by the French Revolution, and new numbers by the Industrial Revolution. Whenever business slumped and food was short, during the war and the post-war depression, they swelled their ranks and perfected their techniques. Their pressure was so great by 1832 that parliamentary reform was at last conceded. The Whigs, fearing revolution, abolished the rotten boroughs and gave the upper-middle class the vote, to save England from democracy.

By that time the power of the crown was only a ghost. The election of 1834 showed that the king could no longer guarantee a majority for the ministers of his choice. He had lost his patronage; and this was due, not to the Economic Reforms of Burke and the Rockingham Whigs, but to the administrative reforms of Pitt—George III's choice, and idol of the Tories. In the interests of economy and efficiency, he initiated changes in government departments which were quietly continued by succeeding ministries. Public officials began to receive regular salaries, instead of making what they could out of fees and perquisites. Their appointment and promotion began to depend on merit rather than political connection. Similar streamlining occurred in the armed forces and the Church. Industrialised England fighting revolutionary France could no longer afford the incompetence and waste of government by favouritism; but the substitution of civil servants for 'placemen' was transforming the political scene.

Other forces were pushing in the same direction. George III's insanity meant a stronger Prime Minister; and Pitt's grip over his cabinet and House of Commons was firmer than that of any previous minister. Moreover, politics was ceasing to be solely concerned with foreign affairs, and was becoming what it is now: a matter of Commissions of Enquiry, and White Papers and

House of Commons

Acts of Parliament. Industrial growth and the massing of the population made it impossible to leave social problems to the initiative of the Justices and the borough councillors. The result was that governments could no longer deal with problems as they came along, facing parliament now and then, when extra sailors for the navy, or a subsidy for a German elector needed its consent. Prime Ministers from Pitt onwards had programmes, and they needed steady majorities to put them into legislative form. And this involved the slow construction of parties, based on principle rather than patronage. The placemen were dwindling; and so were the independents, as they were drawn into one side of the battle or the other. Later Georgian England was taking the first steps towards the two-party system of Victorian times.

The little world of Georgian politics was thus expanding beyond the king and his circle of grandees. The radical movement showed that the electorate, and the masses outside that, were no longer content to sit quietly while their destinies were decided for them far above their heads. The middle classes were expanding; and at least the skilled section of the working classes was getting enough education to read parliamentary debates and government reports, as well as the newspapers, themselves being industrialised. England was far from democracy, but the welfare of the people could no longer be ignored by those in power.

Political theory was also increasingly concerned with alleviating human suffering; a perhaps not unexpected culmination of an era which regarded life as a search for happiness, with reason as the guide. The Dissenters proved very fertile in speculation. Having no orthodoxy to defend, they were drawn into some very adventurous thinking; while Churchmen sought more subtle ways of defending the status quo. Even a Watson, whose refusal to become a government scribe condemned him to a lifetime on the bottom rung of the episcopal ladder, could preach a sermon on 'The Wisdom and Goodness of God in having made both rich and poor'. In contrast, Richard Price and Joseph Priestley, both Dissenting ministers, were prominent theorists in the radical movement from Wilkes' time onward. Starting

150

from an emphasis on the natural rights side of Locke, these radicals reached some very democratic conclusions, by deductive methods which sometimes led them astray from the observable behaviour of man in society. The deist, Tom Paine, though a practising revolutionary in America and in France, followed the same rationalist route in the *Rights of Man*. 'In order to gain a clear and just idea of the design and end of government,' he said, 'let us suppose a small number of persons settled in

Tom Paine

some sequestered part of the earth.' But the most thoroughgoing pursuit of pure reason is to be found in William Godwin's *Political Justice*, which so inspired Wordsworth, Coleridge and Shelley. Godwin, the son and grandson of Dissenting ministers, had a congregation at Stowmarket till reason and the *philosophes* led him into atheism. Convinced that reason would lead to the reign of virtue were it not for the corrupting influence of social and political institutions, he proposed to abolish them all, and build society afresh in the light of naked reason. With his bold free-thinking, his high moral tone and his exciting optimism, he is the culmination of the Age of Reason, before its hopes were blasted by the failure of the French revolutionaries to live up to them.

The great break with this rationalist tradition was made by Burke, whose writings on aesthetics, morals and politics are filled with that awareness of the value of feeling, instinct and tradition, which was also revolutionising literature and the arts. This supporter of the Americans in 1776, and hammer of George III, broke with Fox over the French Revolution, and with his *Reflections* became the founder of modern conservatism. Even George III said that it was 'a good book, a very good book, and every gentleman ought to read it'. Burke preferred the ancient institutions which had slowly evolved through history to the blueprints of the abstract calculators. 'The science of constructing a commonwealth, or renovating it, or reforming it, is,

like every other experimental science, not to be taught *a priori.'*
With his feet firmly on the ground of day-to-day politics, he had
a profound appreciation of the complexity of human nature and
society. 'Politics', he said, 'ought to be adjusted, not to human
reasonings, but to human nature; of which the reason is but a
part, and by no means the greatest part.' For better or worse,
Burke's pragmatism has affected the growth of English institutions ever since.

INDUSTRY

The politicians were now having to face new problems thrown
up by the runaway industrial growth which began in the 'eighties
and which was bound up, in ways not fully understood, with the
growth of the population. This latter phenomenon is probably
the most powerful of the forces which were wrecking the Georgian way of life, but, unfortunately, its causes are far from clear.
Whether it was mainly due to a fall in the death-rate, or a
rise in the birth-rate, or a combination of the two, is still an
open question; particularly as we are not very sure exactly
what these rates were. The falling death-rate was probably
due to a number of factors: better food-supply, and better
housing; the decline in gin-drinking and the increase in the
supply of soap; the paving and draining of the streets; the
wearing of easily washable cottons instead of woollens;
inoculation, vaccination and many other medical advances.
Perhaps the ravages of disease in the middle years of the
century produced a more resistant population later; perhaps the
diseases themselves became less virulent.

And the fall in the death-rate probably increased the population less by adding to the numbers of surviving adults than by
preserving from death children and adolescents who would
later have children. In other words, the death-rate acted via the
birth-rate. And the latter, of course, was affected by other factors.
The improved standard of living may have increased fertility.
The improvements in transport helped, for would-be husbands
and wives were given a wider area of choice, and many found
partners who would have remained unmarried earlier in the
century. This is one of the ways in which the Industrial Revolution

Marriage ceremony

impinges on the population rise. Another is the breakdown of the apprenticeship system which encouraged people to marry earlier. The changes on the land had the same effect, by eliminating the cottagers and increasing the size of farms. This process swelled the ranks of the farm-labourers, who now married and settled in cottages, instead of living in the farmers' households as bachelors. The quickening economic activity may have encouraged workers to have more children by making it easier to feed and clothe them. Or, as Arthur Young thought, by providing jobs for them. 'Away! my boys', he said, 'get children, they are worth more than ever they were.'

Whatever the causes, the population graph took wing in the 'eighties, and soared upwards through the nineteenth century. And, in its turn, it was one of the important stimulants of economic growth. It increased production by extending the demand for goods; and it made this feasible by supplying the necessary labour. During the 'twenties, 'thirties and 'forties, shortage of skilled labour had been one of the causes of the slowing down of that business activity which had been so buoyant since late Stuart times. It was nothing strange in the eighteenth century to find employers desperately searching for staff in one part of the country, and widespread unemployment near by. The mobility of labour was, of course, reduced by the poor-law system and by the inadequate transport arrangements; but, apart from that, the Georgian worker was not one to move automatically to higher wages, or to work as regularly or as long as possible. That was the Victorian worker, and he was not yet born; or, rather, he had not been made.

One of the tasks of the first generations of industrial entrepreneurs was to create a labour force out of intractable material. The lower classes, before the factories came, were used to the greater freedom and easier rhythm of farming or domestic industry. The farm-labourer worked long hours in the summer, and enjoyed a great deal of leisure in the winter. The weaver working in his own home could take his own decisions about when to work and when to rest. And irregular habits were encouraged by an economic system which went by fits and starts, according to the season, the weather, the fashion, the trade-cycle or the cycle of war and peace. Weavers often left their looms to get the harvest in. The fulling-mills of Yorkshire often closed down in summer for lack of water. London house-painters and plasterers could only work in the summer, while the best people were away. When the Season began in the autumn, they were thrown out of work. The result was, according to a writer in the 'forties, that 'the journeymen of this branch are the dirtiest, laziest, and most debauched set of fellows there are of any trade in and about London'.

Intemperate habits were partly due to the irregularity of pay of those who were working. Ambrose Crowley's iron-works was unusual in paying its workers regularly every week. Farm workers were paid annually; servants quarterly; employees in the domestic system every two or three months; casual labourers when they had finished the job. Moreover, living conditions were getting easier, especially in the middle decades when food was cheap, and labourers tended to put in half a week or so to earn enough to live on, and then opt for leisure in the alehouse for the remainder. 'When wages are good', said Defoe, 'they won't work any more than from hand to mouth; or if they do work they spend it in riot or luxury.'

Neither that type of worker, nor the self-employed weaver or file-smith or smallholder found it easy to adjust himself to the relentless regularity of the machine; and many preferred starvation in their own village to the nightmare of the town. Factory work was regarded as the last stage of degradation, in spite of the higher wages, and the type of migrant worker who submitted to it was not very malleable material. The employers resorted to a number of devices to instil discipline. Samuel Oldknow had a system of fines to cut down 'the horrid and impious Vice of the profane CURSING and SWEARING [to quote a notice in his works]—and the Habits of Losing Time,—and DRUNKENNESS'. Men were often hired by the year, and then the law could be brought to bear on recalcitrants. One runaway from Cromford was given a month's hard labour in the house of correction at Derby, 'he being charged by Mr. Arkwright, Cotton-Merchant, with having absented himself from his Masters Business without Leave, (being a hired Servant for a Year) and likewise been guilty of divers Misdemenors and Misbehaviour'.

Some employers were slave-drivers, but the incidence of that type has been exaggerated. In any case, it was not the way to get results. Successful entrepreneurs like Boulton were wiser in their approach. 'I have trained up many, and am training up more, plain country lads into good workmen', he said. Arkwright usually took a patriarchal line with his people, and used the carrot as well as the stick. At Cromford he ran an annual festival when his workers were regaled with food and drink, music and dancing. 'This makes them industrious and sober all the rest of the year', wrote one diarist who saw it. Arkwright also gave bonuses to his most deserving workers, and in 1783, according to the *Derby Mercury*, he gave 'to 27 of his principal Workmen, Twenty-Seven fine Milch Cows, worth from 8£ to 10£ each'. Some of the early industrial centres had an air of the feudal village about them, with the factory-owner as the almighty squire.

Carpenter

One of the difficulties of recruiting labour, particularly in the textile areas, was that most of the men were only required in the initial stages of building the mill and setting up the machinery. After that, the bulk of the employees were women and children. When Arkwright began his second mill at Cromford, he advertised: 'Wanted . . . Forging & Filing Smiths, Joiners and Carpenters, Framework-Knitters and Weavers, with large Families. Likewise Children of all Ages, above

155

seven years old, may have constant Employment.' As we have seen, there was nothing new in the employment of children. Childhood as we know it, as a special age with its own needs and customs, did not exist in the Georgian lower classes. It had to be invented in the nineteenth century; just as we have created in the twentieth century a new age, unheard of before—the 'teenage'. Writers like Defoe expressed pleasure at seeing children making their contribution almost as soon as they could walk: it was a sign of a healthy economy. The factories employed children along with their parents as well as binding pauper apprentices. Some of them imported whole batches of poor children from London parishes; and they were probably no worse off in a Lancashire factory than they would have been tied to a metro-politan chimney-sweep.

Children were preferred to adults because they were cheaper. Moreover, since their minds were still pliable, they were easier than their fathers to mould into good industrial labour. The new middle class thus had an enormous influence over the forma-tion of the new working man. And this educational process was not limited to the 12 hours or so that the children worked in the factory each day (or night), but extended to Sunday as well. Strutt built a Unitarian chapel at Belper, and Arkwright began an Anglican church at Cromford. And all the employers were warm supporters of the Sunday School movement, which began in 1780 and spread rapidly in the next decades. Strutt opened one for his cotton-workers at Belper, and earned the praises

Children in a rope factory

of the *Derby Mercury* for his 'Liberality which does Honour to the human Heart'. 'It becomes the Duty of every thinking Person', added the article, 'in this Age of Refinement, Luxury, and Vice, to hold forth an assisting Hand, to stop the Tide of Immorality, which threatens speedily to Deluge "The Land of Liberty".'

It was when the lower classes began to mass together in the new industrial areas that the upper ranks began to realise that they were sitting on a moral and political volcano. The guns of the Evangelical movement were trained on this problem, and probably the Sunday Schools were the most effective weapon of all. Robert Raikes, the owner of the *Gloucester Journal*, who provided the initial drive for the movement, described its effect on working children in his town. 'From being idle, ungovernable, profligate, and filthy in the extreme, they say the boys and girls are become not only cleanly and decent in appearance, but are greatly humanised in their manners— more orderly, tractable and attentive to business.' It was partly by such measures as these, and partly by stern police action, that the Georgian ruling classes managed to survive the testing times when industrialisation, French Revolutionary ideas and the crises of a war-time economy converged to shake society to its very foundations.

Some contemporaries, of course, felt that the education of the poor was exactly the wrong way to maintain 'subordination'. One sceptic was the Hon. John Byng, who, speaking of the Sunday Schools, wrote: 'I am point-blank against these institutions; the poor should not read, and of writing I never learnt, for them, the use.' And Richard Guest, looking back from just after the end of our period, hit the nail on the head when he wrote: 'The operative workmen being thrown together in great numbers, had their faculties sharpened and improved by constant communication.' 'They took a greater interest in the defeats and victories of their country's arms', he added, 'from being only a few degrees above their cattle in the scale of intellect, they became political citizens.' In the long run, then, John Byng's fears were justified.

157

Coach leaving the Turf Hotel, Newcastle

CULTURE

While they were teaching the workers to read, the middle classes were sending their own children to school, and improving their own minds with circulating libraries and Literary and Philosophical societies. A mass readership was coming into being which had lasting effects on Augustan culture. And improved transport quickened the process. 'A new fashion', said Sir John Hawkins, 'pervades the whole of this our island almost as instantaneously as a spark of fire illuminates a mass of gunpowder.' But it was not only clothes. Every department of cultural life now served a national market, as ideas spread down through the classes, and across through the provinces. Nor was it a one-way traffic, for writers and artists could not be indifferent to the wants of their new audience.

'The author, when unpatronized by the Great,' wrote Goldsmith, 'has naturally recourse to the bookseller. There cannot be, perhaps, imagined a combination more prejudicial to taste than this.' He was right about Georgian taste. The various ingredients of the Romantic movement are visible from the 'forties onwards. In Fielding, there was a warm sympathy for humanity, based on the heart not the head. Richardson's novels exploited sentiment and explored feelings. Poets shifted their emphasis from the general to the particular, from society to the individual, from the normal to the unusual. In Thomson, Shenstone, Young and Collins, tenderness, pity, melancholy and mystery add new dimensions to verse. And this cultivation of the emotions and probing of the heart mark a break with the Augustan tradition, which believed with Johnson that the influence of the passions 'is uniform, and their effects nearly the same in every human breast: a man loves and hates, desires

158

and avoids, exactly like his neighbour'. Moreover, the rigidity of verse-forms was weakened, the rules were broken, language became softer, and its object was to cast a spell rather than to make a point.

Visible also, in many forms, is a desire to move away from the urban sophistication of Georgian life. Cowper celebrated the simple pleasures of country life. He had a keen eye for the beauties of nature. And so did Thomson, who passed from simply describing scenery to imbuing it with emotions. 'He describes not to the eye alone', wrote Hazlitt, 'but to the other senses, and to the whole man. He puts his heart into his subject, writes as he feels, and humanises whatever he touches.' Gray escaped into History; Beckford in *Vathek* to oriental romance; Walpole in the *Castle of Otranto* to medieval horror; and Percy to his *Reliques of Ancient English Poetry*.

The steady assurance of Georgian literature was also endangered by shifts in the intellectual sub-soil. A number of writers found that reason could not bear the weight that the eighteenth century placed on it. A strong tradition through Shaftesbury, Burke and Adam Smith based ethics on moral sentiments rather than on rational calculations. And with Hume reason itself dug its own grave. Moreover, the Methodists and the rest of the Evangelicals were rousing support by appeals to the heart not the head. And England, like the rest of Europe, came under the spell of Rousseau,

Charles Towneley in his library

whose *Nouvelle Héloïse* and *Emile* were charged with emotion; and of the German philosophers, who were drowning empiricism in oceans of intuition, illumination and faith.

In the end came the French Revolution which was decisive. The generation of Wordsworth and Coleridge were intoxicated with joy at this opportunity for men to create the perfect society, based on justice and equality, and shorn of the evils that reason found in Georgian life. But with the excesses of the Terror and the aggressions of French nationalism, the dream became a nightmare. They awoke to the realisation that pure reason could lead to unadulterated evil, and rational ethics to a moral vacuum.

Their disappointment was intense. Coleridge wrote that he had withdrawn from 'French metaphysics, French politics, French ethics, and French theology'. In the same year, 1798, he and Wordsworth published the first edition of their *Lyrical Ballads,* poetical experiments, designed, they said, 'to ascertain how far the language of conversation in the middle and lower classes of society is adapted to the purposes of poetic pleasure'. They wished to make a clean break with the artificialities and proprieties of Augustan verse, which had become, in Cowper's earlier phrase, 'a mere mechanic art'. They also broke with Georgian society in favour of 'humble and rustic life', as they said in 1800, 'because, in that condition, the essential passions of the heart find a better soil in which they can attain their maturity, are less under restraint, and speak a plainer and more emphatic language'. Above all, they wished to live close to nature. 'I love fields and woods and mountains', said Coleridge, 'with almost a visionary fondness.' And this was not the nature of the Georgian writers: the attractive background to urban life and pleasant relief from social sophistication. The Romantics responded to nature with rapture. They felt that its close presence would soothe their anguish and teach them the deepest truths about life itself.

We have here the evolution of a new concept of the artist and his place in society. In fact, during these years the word 'art' acquired its present meaning. What it meant to Georgians a few years before comes out in a letter Thomas Jefferson wrote home while visiting England: 'I could write you volumes on the improvements which I find made, and making here, in the arts. One deserves particular notice ... the application of steam as an agent for working grist mills.' Wordsworth, on the other hand, asked, 'What is a Poet?'; and answered that he was a man 'endowed with more lively sensibility, more enthusiasm and tenderness, who has a greater knowledge of human nature, and a more comprehensive soul, than are supposed to be common among mankind'. With his heightened perception and visionary imagination he reveals truths about ultimate reality; and is thus rated far above his Augustan pre-

William Blake

decessors, who told us, though in a very diverting way, what we knew already.

'Imagination is My World; this world of Dross is beneath my notice.' So wrote Blake, who swung even more violently away from the Age of Reason into visions and mysticism. Reynolds had lectured: 'in the midst of the highest flights of fancy or imagination, reason ought to preside from first to last'. Blake replied: 'If this is true, it is a devilish foolish thing to be an artist.' And elsewhere he wrote: '"What", it will be questioned, "When the sun rises, do you not see a round disc of fire somewhat like a guinea?" O no, no, I see an innumerable company of the heavenly host crying, "Holy, Holy, Holy is the Lord God Almighty".'

Painting did not escape the restlessness which was disturbing Georgian life in all its aspects. After mid-century, taste began to shift from formal portraits and conversation-pieces to the landscapes of Claude, Gaspar Poussin and Salvator Rosa. Craggy mountains and steep precipices, hanging woods and cascading torrents were now in demand—the grand and the sublime. The young gentlemen were even enjoying the Alps on the way to Italy; the Lake District found its admirers; and gardeners like 'Capability' Brown were given orders to remould the view from the Palladian window to make it look like a picture. Native talent continued to be neglected. Richard Wilson's 'picturesque' treatment of English and Welsh scenes in the Italian manner found little support. He died a poor man, unmentioned in the newspapers. Nor was typically English scenery appreciated at this stage. 'Our ever-verdant lawns', wrote Walpole, 'rich vales, fields and haycocks and hop grounds are neglected as homely and familiar objects.' Gainsborough died with his house stacked with unsold landscapes. These were not appreciated till the very end of this period; and then, with the Romantic movement, we find the greatest talent painting, not faces or 'elevated' landscapes, but nature itself.

Similarly, the Palladian 'rule of taste' was coming to an end in building. As architects became more emancipated socially, they grew less subservient artistically, and a variety of styles emerged. The chameleon-like James Wyatt, who could run up a building in any style required, typifies the fragmentation of taste that marks the end of the Georgian era. His Pantheon, the new fashionable assembly-rooms in Oxford Street, was a version of the church of Sancta Sophia at Constantinople. His Fonthill, designed to satisfy the Romantic taste of Beckford, rose at first as an artificial ruin. Later it was elaborated into a great mansion looking like a Gothic cathedral.

Fonthill Abbey, Wiltshire

The Augustans had despised Gothic: it was uncivilised and against reason. Addison was impressed by the 'prodigious pains and expenses that our forefathers have been at in these barbarous buildings'; and wondered 'what miracles of architecture they would have

Strawberry Hill (1753–78)

left us had they only been instructed in the right way'. On the other hand, churches and colleges, and other buildings in the Gothic style, were going up all through the century. Vanbrugh, when designing Blenheim, wanted to leave part of the old manor of Woodstock standing. Later architects *built* ruins, especially when the mode of the 'picturesque' came in. Though, as Gilpin, the expert on this subject, remarked, 'It is not every man who can build a house that can execute a ruin. To give a stone its mouldering appearance—to make the widening chink run naturally through all the joints—to mutilate the ornaments.'

Ruins clearly took some building; but Horace Walpole was even more elaborate with his whimsy. Strawberry Hill was built by various friends over a long period, and its studied irregularity was supposed to simulate the chaotic growth of medieval structures. And in the last decades of the period, what had begun as an eccentricity turned into an earnest pursuit. Buildings like Lacock Abbey and Downton Castle suited the mood of a generation anxious to break loose from Georgian rules into other worlds. Nash, before his Regency days, was an expert in castellated mansions and ornamental cottages. 'Chinoiserie' was another symptom of the same break-up; and so were the balconies and verandas in the Indian style. The Royal Pavilion at Brighton was not far away.

MORALS

One final metamorphosis must be mentioned: these decades saw the Georgian ethos change into Victorian middle-class morality. The Methodist and Evangelical movements had been spreading with inspired energy among sections of the middle classes, and making an impressive mark on the lower orders. Nevertheless, the unsettling of the traditional order of society by industrialisation made it appear that vice was gaining. 'High and low, cobblers, tinkers, hackney coachmen, men and maid servants, soldiers, tradesmen of all ranks, lawyers,

163

physicians, gentlemen, lords', wrote Wesley in 1782, 'are as ignorant of the Creator of the world as Mohametans or Pagans.' He was unduly pessimistic, for at this very time an extraordinary phenomenon was occurring: puritanism began to receive powerful recruits from the *haut monde*. The reasons why the upper classes began to look to their morals are complex. The intense pressure of a buoyant manufacturing class is one factor. The transfer of the economic centre of gravity to the provinces and the north is another. The concentrations of godless proletarians made the ruling class uneasy, especially after such nightmares as the Gordon Riots. But, undoubtedly, the French Revolution clinched the matter. The collapse of the *Ancien Régime* under violent atheism sent a chill down patrician spines; and the long war that England fought against an iconoclastic enemy continued the shock treatment.

Whatever the reasons, old Georgian reprobates began to wilt under the frowns of their children and grandchildren. Some took no notice, like old grandfather Wilberforce who said, 'If Billy turns Methodist, he shall not have sixpence of mine'. Some indulged in the even wilder extravagances that we associate with the Regency. But most of the upper classes had at least to appear to support the new standards, and many were genuinely converted, like the Duke of Grafton. This old rake from the 'sixties wrote a pamphlet in the 'eighties on the theme that there could be no improvement in morals till the superior classes mended their ways.

The key convert was William Wilberforce. As the son of a rich commercial family in Hull, M.P. for Yorkshire and frequenter of the most exclusive social circles, he was able to exert a powerful influence in high places. He was also the leader of the Clapham Sect, the general staff of the whole Evangelical campaign. This group of wealthy philanthropists lived at Clapham Common, just outside London, where John Venn, son of one of the first Evangelicals, was vicar, and Henry Thornton the banker was patron of the living. Their impetus was behind most of the drives of this period, from the Anti-Slavery Society to the Sunday School movement.

The war on vice was waged on many fronts. In 1787, after

persuading George III to publish a proclamation against various forms of immorality, Wilberforce formed the Proclamation Society, which set to work on the lines of the old Society for the Reformation of Manners. In 1802, this was absorbed into the more powerful Society for the Suppression of Vice, which came down heavily on Sabbath-breaking, swearing, brothel-keeping and using false weights and measures. The inn-keepers of Margate were warned that their licences would be suspended if they hired out their premises for masquerades. At Brighton, a notice went up threatening gentlemen's servants with prosecution if they bathed in the nude. The Rev. Sydney Smith, a Georgian survivor, called it 'a society for suppressing the vices of persons whose income does not exceed £500 per annum'.

Wilberforce received mighty assistance from Hannah More, the former bluestocking, successful playwright and friend of Johnson and Garrick. Now converted, she too realised the urgent necessity of purifying upper-class life. Her pamphlets, *Thoughts upon the Importance of the Manners of the Great*, and *An Estimate of the Religion of the Fashionable World*, went into several editions

Recreation inside the Fleet Prison

Hannah More

in the 'nineties. Following Raikes' example, she and her sisters founded a Sunday School in Cheddar, and then a dozen others in the area. The success of these and others all over the country meant that more children were learning to read than ever before. Sceptics still thought that this was playing with fire, especially with the levelling and deistical writings of Tom Paine circulating so widely. She herself said that 'to teach the poor to read without providing them with safe books has always appeared to me as a dangerous measure'. And, consequently, she launched her *Cheap Repository* of monthly tracts, which reached a circulation of two million a year. These moral tales and verses spread the Evangelical message to all classes. The *Roguish Miller*, who cheated his customers, finally landed in gaol. In *The Story of Sinful Sally*, the heroine took her first step down the slippery slope by becoming a kept woman, and then suffered moral collapse after reading novels. The ballad called *The Riot, or half a Loaf is Better than No Bread* is said to have quelled two bread riots in the famine year of 1795.

So powerful was her voice on behalf of loyalty in Church and State, that the Religious Tract Society was founded to extend the campaign. A few years later, leading Evangelicals of all denominations formed the British and Foreign Bible Society. Appealling for funds from the 'rich and middle ranks', the *Christian Observer* said, 'By what other means can you contribute so essentially to the preservation of order, to authority of the law, and the stability of government?' It was therefore 'a matter of policy as well as of duty, to create an interest among the lower classes for the possession and perusal of the sacred records'.

Unfortunately, there is no room here to examine certain aspects of this vast campaign, for example, the work of the

Society for Bettering the Condition and Increasing the Comforts of the Poor, or the Society for Promoting the Observance of the Sabbath. The government's work in suppressing seditious literature and locking up radicals must be passed over; and we can only glance at the efforts of private persons to expurgate the body of English literature. Shakespeare was emasculated and rewritten years before Bowdler took to his scissors. 'Barefaced obscenities, low vulgarity, and nauseous vice so frequently figure and pollute his pages', wrote a leading Methodist preacher, 'that we cannot but lament the luckless hour in which he became a writer for the stage.' Authors like Addison or Richardson, who had written in their day with moralising motives, were too indelicate to place in the hands of later-Georgian young ladies.

These changes are but part of that vast shift in outlook which has affected English society down to the present day. As a result of it, slaves were liberated in the colonies and children were chained to machines in the factories. Moral earnestness produced the upright public servant along with the tyrannical husband and father; the mutilation of the classics along with the sublimest of poetry. Hypocrisy coincided with the clear-eyed pursuit of scientific truth; humanitarianism with the harshest of penal codes. Increased control over nature promised an end to immemorial poverty, while reducing thousands to misery. The Georgian era left problems of the direst kind; but the productive capacity, the political institutions and the moral force to solve them were Georgian products no less. 'What has rendered England the wonder and envy of

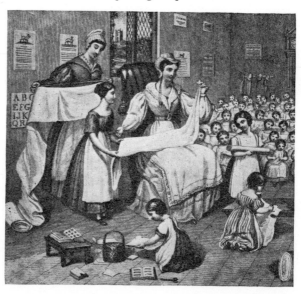

Improving the poor

Europe?', Horace Walpole once asked. His answer was: 'Freedom'.

Further Reading

Asa Briggs, *The Age of Improvement*, 1959.
Boris Ford (ed.), *The Pelican Guide to English Literature*, Vol. 5: *From Blake to Byron*, 1957.
M. J. Quinlan, *Victorian Prelude*, 1941.
G. Rattray Taylor, *The Angel-makers*, 1958.
Steven Watson, *Reign of George III*, 1960.

Index

*Figures in **bold type** refer to pages on which illustrations appear*